COOPER AND PACKRAT

Mystery
of the
Eagle's Nest

By Tamra Wight

Illustrations by Carl DiRocco

ISLANDPORT PRESS

ISLANDPORT PRESS

ISLANDPORT PRESS
P. O. Box 10
Yarmouth, Maine 04096
www.islandportpress.com
books@islandportpress.com

ISBN: 978-1-939017-35-2
Library of Congress Control Number: 2013922660
Printed in the USA

Dean L. Lunt, Publisher
Front and back cover art: Carl DiRocco
Book jacket design: Karen Hoots / Hoots Design
Book design: Michelle Lunt / Islandport Press

For David, Alex, and Ben
for oh, so very many reasons

Chapter 1

Eagles mostly eat fish, but will steal both live and dead food from other eagles or birds of prey, such as osprey or heron.

There were only three ways to get to the floor of the super-cool canyon in my family's woods. One: You could jump the twelve feet down, but you'd probably break your neck; and two: You could follow the brook flowing along the north side and jump down the waterfall into a not-so-deep pool of water. Either way, if you could still walk, then you'd have to go a hundred yards downriver, before squeezing through a wicked narrow gorge at the back of the canyon.

Or, three: You could use the secret entrance.

My back against a tree trunk, I carefully leaned out and around to peek back the way I'd come. Darn it! The two humongous men who'd been chasing me were now trying to cross the swollen brook. *I* knew how to pick stepping-stones; the higher and drier, the better. But these suit-and-tie goons were obviously not the hiking type. About halfway across, blue-tie guy stepped on a dark green rock with his shiny black shoes. Not a good combination. He leaned left, then right, then back to the left before grabbing red-tie guy's arm. The two of them wiggled on their rocks, swearing like crazy, arms waving so fast I thought they'd take off like a duck who'd just been surprised by a guy in a camouflage suit. Finally, red-tie guy shook off blue-tie guy.

After getting their balance back, they stood perfectly still for a second, looked at each other, and laughed. Then, *whoosh!* Their feet slid out from under them. Lying on their backs in the middle of the brook, they swore between groans as they slowly rolled over and tried to stand.

It was the break I needed.

Cooper and Packrat: Mystery of the Eagle's Nest

Creeping along the edge of the canyon, I tried to keep the pine tree between the goons' line of sight and me. I parted two blueberry bushes to drop my green, plastic geocache box into the hole between them. When it clunked on the rock floor six feet below, I winced and peeked back at the goons.

They were still arguing. *Whew.*

I put my feet in the hole, gave three chickadee calls so my friend Packrat would know I'd made it, then wiggled my waist through. As I balanced on my elbows, I looked for a foothold with the tip of my left hiking boot. It slipped on the damp dirt. Surprised, I just let go and my bare knee scraped the wall as I dropped the last couple of feet to land in a crouch. The bushes sprang back into place above me, blocking out most of the light.

The canyon opened up before me. I was still a good five feet up from the floor, and I knew from experience that the only way anyone would find me was if they laid on their stomach above me, slid forward, and hung over the edge. As long as I didn't do something stupid like sneeze, I was pretty safe here.

I was breathing hard, blood rushing through my veins. After my mad dash through the woods, my heart was pounding so loud, I couldn't think. *Why the heck did those guys want my geocache box so badly?* They'd crashed through the woods just as Packrat and I had reached the coordinates for one of our caches, the one hidden in the old stone wall. Next thing we knew, they'd started swearing and running toward us! When their coats flapped open, I could've sworn I saw a gun in their waistbands. Thinking back, I wasn't really sure. But I do remember grabbing the box and running like a deer. Yeah, I knew right away it was a pretty stupid thing to do. It made them keep chasing us. So I held the rectangular box over my head, hoping the goons would follow me, while signaling Packrat to go around the long way in case he had to go for backup.

I squatted next to the long, skinny box. It was one of six just like it, all hidden in different spots along a trail that my friends and I had made this spring. The trail began and ended at Wilder Family Campground, the campground on Pine Lake that my family owned and where we lived all year long. Each box held a small notebook with a pen, to log in the date you'd found the box, and some cheap plastic toy prizes for younger hikers. There were six more boxes, much smaller ones—no bigger than a matchbox, really. These had only a mini golf-type pencil and some scrolled-up paper to log in on; these were harder and more fun to find.

All twelve of these geocache boxes were camouflaged to blend in with the woods. Packrat and Roy (my two best friends, both seasonal campers at our campground) and I had searched high and low for cool places to hide them, like hollow trees and dark holes between rocks. People who wanted to hike the trail and look for the boxes could rent a handheld GPS from Mom in our campground office. The GPS can tell you exactly where you are on the planet. We had entered the latitude and longitude coordinates for all twelve geocache boxes into the GPS device, to get hikers within twenty-five feet of each one. From there, they had to use our written clues to find the actual box. Once they logged in, they closed the box up tight and hid the container back in the same exact spot for the next geocacher. It was kinda like a high-tech hide-and-seek game.

Just last week, I'd checked this box's hiding spot, and all the usual stuff had been in it. I'd thrown in a few campground postcards to add to the prizes, and replaced the pencil that had gotten stubby.

I didn't get it. *Why had these goons chased me?* I reached a shaky hand toward the large clip on its skinny side.

"Where'd he go?" asked one of the goons, his voice above me.

I froze. *Breathe slow,* I told myself. *Don't move.*

"I don't know! I swear he was standing right here a minute ago."

"Ha! Maybe we scared him to death and he jumped off the side."

They walked back and forth along the edge above me, just like Packrat and I had done when we'd found the place and were looking for a way down. I slowly stood up as dirt, pine needles, and last fall's brown leaves fell in front of my face, into the canyon. The goons stopped. Their shoe tips hung over the edge. I prayed they'd slip on moss and fall. I imagined the look on their faces as they passed by the ledge, seeing me safe and sound with the box. I'd smile. Maybe wave.

"You see him?" said a goon.

"Nah. Let's go follow the brook down, get a look at the bottom of this thing."

"Are you crazy? We almost broke our necks trying to cross it! Besides, he headed this way; I saw him."

"You're just sore 'cause you got your new shoes wet."

"Shut up, you."

Neither one said a word as they walked back and forth again, trying to find a way down. After a couple of minutes, I heard a frustrated groan right before a short log flew over the edge. I watched it land on the water-soaked canyon floor with a splat.

"We lost him. And I don't know about you, but there's no way I could pick him out of a lineup."

"You idiot! It's us who'll be in the lineup if we don't find him. Either of them!"

"Those kids took off so fast, Mikey! A blur of shirts is all I saw. One was red—no, wait, brownish. Maybe maroon? And orange. Yeah. The other was definitely orange."

I heard a sigh from Mikey, the one I now thought of as the smarter of the two.

"And we're dead, you know," continued the dumb one. "When the boss finds out we let a couple of kids get those parts, we're dead."

I picked up the box. *The parts?*

Mikey spoke up. "Well, whose idea was it for us to stuff them in a box, hide it in the woods, and tell the buyer to make a switch with the cash? Huh?"

"You agreed to it! It was a great plan. The buyer wouldn't see us, and we wouldn't see him. How was I supposed to know there'd be another box out here? And that the buyer would grab the wrong one!"

"It would have been a great plan if you'd remembered to put the tracking device on the box; then we would've known exactly where to find those parts. But now the buyer doesn't have the parts. We don't have the parts. Some bratty kids have the parts!"

The dumb one started whining again. "Cement blocks are gonna be tied to our feet when the boss finds out. We'll be dropped in the lake! We're dead, Mikey. Dead as—"

"Would you shut up already about being dead? We'll just explain what happened. Tell the boss—"

"Hey! What's that?"

More dirt rained down and I backed up as far as I could until my back met the cool earth. The geocache box felt like a hot potato in my hands.

"Over there. By that big tree."

The two sets of heavy footfalls became fainter as they walked away. I looked down at myself. By the tree? Did I drop something? My geocache GPS? No, it was still around my neck. Backup compass? Utility knife? Notebook? Water bottle?

It was all still here. What could they—

"Hey, it's a pen! Do ya think it still writes? It's a nice one. I like fat pens, you know, 'cause I have big hands and—"

"Gimme that!"

"Hey, *I* found it! Finders weepers and all that stuff. Besides, it has a moose on it, see? And my nickname's Moose."

No, no, no, no! I checked my pocket, groaned out loud, then slapped a hand over my mouth. My pen. My Wilder Family Campground pen.

"I think," said Mikey—and I swear I heard a smile in his voice—"we're going camping."

Chapter 2

Many years ago, bald eagles were hunted for sport.
They were also killed to protect livestock and fishing
spots. As a result, eagles almost became extinct. It's
been illegal to hunt them since 1940.

After the goons crashed their way through the trees and brush, back toward the way they'd come, I heard three barn owl hoots in a row and answered with my chickadee call. *Chick-a-dee-dee-dee!*

Packrat peeked out from the narrow gorge on the floor at the other end of the canyon. I raised my arm to give the all-clear signal, and he raised his in return to say he'd be right over.

I attached the geocache box to my backpack strap with a utility clip. Then I reached out from the cave, leapt to a pine-tree trunk, and shimmied down. I waved Packrat over to my right, toward another small cave opening. This one was on the ground level, so we'd have something to duck into if those goons doubled back to look down on the canyon.

"We're in big trouble," I whispered. Putting the geocache box on the ground, I filled him in on everything the bad guys had said about losing their stuff, and what their boss would think.

"So, they chased us 'cause they thought we had *their* box?" Packrat stared at it like it'd grown horns and legs. "But it was hidden at *our* geocache coordinates! Kind of." He took a deep breath, and slowly let it out. "It wasn't in the exact same spot, but the finders sometimes mess up when they put them back." He sighed. "Okay. So, we just open it up, right? If it has their—what did you say, parts?—it's theirs. If it has our prizes and logbook, then it's ours."

We stared at it. Finally, for the second time in the last ten minutes, I reached out a hand to flip the big latch.

"Wait!" Packrat grabbed my arm to stop me. "I changed my mind. If we don't open it—if we leave it right here," he said, pointing at the ground, "we can honestly say we have no clue what they're talking about if anyone asks us about anything we might or might not have seen out here."

"Are you kidding?" I said. "I have to know! If it's not our stuff, then what was so important that two hulk goons in suits chased us through the woods and are now wicked scared 'cause they lost it?" I shook my head. "Uh-uh. I gotta know. Besides . . . umm . . . they found my pen."

"So?" Packrat said. "A pen isn't—"

"The one with Maxwell Moose on it. And my campground name. And the address."

"*What?!*" Packrat cried.

I ran a hand through my short brown hair. "I know, I know. They did say they didn't get a good look at us." I glanced hopefully at Packrat, but my friend still stared at the geocache box like it would explode any minute. "I want to know what's in there," I insisted. "Don't you? If we know what it is, maybe we can figure out what to do about it. They're tromping through *my* woods. On *our* geocache course."

Packrat stood a little taller. "Yeah. We worked hard to hide all the boxes and make a list of the coordinates—"

"And we made the hiking trail to get to them. We cut brush and marked the way with red spray-paint dots. It took weeks!" I added.

"Those guys were soooooo not campers. That's weird too." Packrat nodded toward the box. "Okay. Go ahead. Do it."

I crouched back down beside the box and took a deep breath. I felt my friend lean over me as I flipped up the big latch on the side. Grabbing the cover, I lifted the long, skinny lid slowly to the left.

Bright yellow eyes stared back at me! *Eagle eyes!* I threw open the lid the rest of the way and scrambled back before realizing the eyes were lifeless.

Packrat gasped. "Is it . . . is it . . . dead?"

Blood pounded through my head, worse than when I'd run away from those goons. Reaching down, I gently pulled out an eagle head attached to a foot-long stick whittled with Native American designs. Blue-colored suede strings were wrapped two or three times around the top of the stick, then hung loosely the rest of the way down. On the strings were red- and yellow-colored beads. Two pairs of claws also lay in the box, along with about twenty loose eagle feathers.

I looked at the fierce, proud face and my stomach turned. A red-hot ball formed inside it, rising slowly through my chest, taking over my brain. Gone was fear. In its place was anger.

"It's just parts," I spat out. "Eagle parts."

"Are they real?" Packrat reached out to hold a feather. "They look so real!"

"I think so." I took a closer look at the eagle head. "I think it's one of those—you know . . . what do they call it when you stuff a real, dead animal?"

"Like a trophy fish on a plaque on a wall." Packrat held the eagle wing, carefully pulling it out, as if the eagle were in flight. His eyes darted to mine in a panic. "Wait, wait, wait! Have you seen *our* eagles lately? This isn't one of the parents, is it?"

I put my fist to my forehead and tapped it, thinking back. "Yester-day. Yesterday morning. Early. Both eagles were on the nest. All three of their eaglets too."

"If someone knew what they were doing, could they kill an eagle one day and put this all together in the box the next?"

I didn't know the answer to that. The eagle head rested in the palm of my hand, the stick reaching just past my elbow. Its eyes stared up at me eerily.

Packrat motioned to the box. "So now that we know, what are we gonna do with it?"

"Well, I'm not giving it back. It's not theirs! They stole it from somebody who's missing it."

"Take it to the warden?"

"She's out of town for a couple of days." I scuffed the tip of my hiking boot through the leaves to the dirt. It was too bad, 'cause Warden Kate had been a big help last summer when one of our campers, a sad misguided man named Mr. Bakeman, had decided the loons on Pine Lake were a nuisance and had tried to get rid of them.

"What if those goons meet us on the way back?" Packrat scanned the ledge above us. "Or what if they're waiting for us at the campground? They'll see we've got the box. They'll make us hand it over."

I studied it. Rectangular in shape. Eighteen inches long, twelve inches high, and six inches wide. Hunter green. One large clip on the right side. A black handle on the top. Side by side with the boxes on our geocache course, you wouldn't know whose was whose. Now I wished we'd painted WILDER FAMILY CAMPGROUND on ours. Or Maxwell Moose's face. But what were the odds some goons would be hiding stolen stuff in our woods?

Packrat gave a small laugh. "Do you suppose the boxes got mixed up? Someone has ours? I'd like to see their face when they open it up and find McDonald's toys and plastic key rings."

"Packrat! That's it!" Suddenly, I knew what we had to do. "We're going to hide this box down here until we know the goons are gone and we can get it to Warden Kate. On the way back, we'll grab another one of our boxes off the trail."

"The one in the old stump is on the way," Packrat suggested.

"If the goons catch up with us before we can turn this one in, we'll show them ours and make them think they chased the wrong box. Got a notebook?" I asked Packrat, even though I already knew the answer.

He dug into one of the many pockets of his detective-style coat. "Yep. And a camera too."

Cooper and Packrat: Mystery of the Eagle's Nest

That coat had been one of the first things I noticed about Pete—his real name—when we met last summer. He and his mom had come to the campground to be near his grandmother, who'd broken her hip. Packrat always wore a long tan trench coat that had tons and tons of pockets, loaded with everything you needed, and then some. When we met, we were both twelve, going into seventh grade. He liked that I was a nature geek and I liked that he was goofy. We'd been best friends ever since.

This year, Packrat and his mom were gonna stay at the campground for the whole summer. School had just ended, and as soon as Packrat's mom had closed up her classroom, they'd moved in to their trailer here. His mom was working for my mom, and Packrat was working for my dad.

I took off my black sweatshirt, the one with our new Wilder Family logo on it, and spread it on the ground. Then I carefully laid the eagle head and stick down on top of it. The head rolled to the left. I turned it beak up. The head rolled to the right.

"Can you hold it?" Packrat asked. I put it back in my palm and laid my arm over the sweatshirt. *Click* went the camera as he took three photos, one from each side.

Laying the head back across the sweatshirt, I set out all the other pieces as well. "You take the photos. I'll write notes about them—all the details and markings."

Packrat leaned his head toward the cave. "Then we'll hide it in there?"

"Yeah," I said. "But I don't want to just leave it on the floor in the open. Let's see if we can find somewhere to hide it—a hole in the wall or something. Just in case someone finds this place by accident."

"But no one knows how to get down here but us," Packrat said, looking up at the rim of the canyon.

"Yeah, and we thought we'd be the only ones to hide geocache boxes on campground property," I said. "Look where that got us."

Chapter 3

Eagles' nests are also called aeries. *On average, the basket-like nests, made of branches and sticks, are six feet in diameter and three feet deep. They are lined with feathers, grasses, pine needles, and moss.*

We were leaving through the gorge. Normally I thought it was cool—how we had to walk sideways, our hands on the stone wall in front of us, our backs and butts sliding along the wall behind, barely squeezing through in some spots. But this time, all I could think about was how there was no way the goons would fit into our little canyon this way, which is what Packrat, Roy, and I called "the easy way." Hiding the cache in it made Packrat and me extra sure those giant goons could never find it.

Thinking of Roy made me smile. I couldn't wait to see my friend's face when we told him about all this. He was gonna be so mad he'd missed it.

Stepping out the other side of the gorge put us into thick woods next to the pool at the bottom of the waterfall. As we followed the brook back to the lake and the spot where we'd dragged our kayaks onto land, we tried to be as quiet as we could, considering we had to stay off the red-blazed trail just in case those goons were following it.

When we reached a giant stump from an old oak that stood about three feet high, I got down on my knees next to it. I held my breath, a little creeped-out about putting my hand in the huge hole under the roots. I felt around in the cool damp dirt, on and under leaves and twigs, until I found the box. As I pulled it out, my breath let go in a *whoosh*.

"One of these times, there's going to be a snake in there," I said.

Packrat dangled a glove in front of my face. I rolled my eyes. "You have to remind me sooner next time!"

I started to stand, but Packrat stopped me. "Open it first! I don't want to lug it back only to find it has more parts."

I did. Seeing our usual cache goodies, I closed the lid and stood to follow my friend. I was so busy watching my feet, I didn't see the branch swing back. *Slap!* The pine needles swatted my face, poking at my skin.

"*Oww!*" I rubbed my cheek, right below my eye.

"Sorry!" Packrat whispered, pointing down at a stick I needed to avoid.

Suddenly, wolf-howl sounds came from my shorts pocket. Packrat ducked down low, while I fumbled to pull out my phone. I knew from the ringtone it was the camp office.

"Hey, Mom?" I half-whispered. "You'll never—"

"Coooop-errrr! You always do that! I'm not Mom."

Packrat stood to look around. Not seeing anything suspicious, he motioned for me to follow him.

"Molly?" I whispered to my five-year-old sister. "Put Mom on, okay?"

Molly started whispering too. "She's got customers. She said I could call you."

Uh-oh. This was bored Molly.

We'd reached a steep, upward embankment. I gave Packrat the box so I could still hold on to the phone and have a free hand to climb. Hand over hand we went. When we reached the top, we slid and skittered down the other side. At the bottom, we bent over to pass under a fallen tree.

The whole time, all Molly did was breathe. Loudly.

"Squirt?" I whisper-asked.

"What?"

"Why'd you call me?" I looked toward Packrat in a she's-being-a-pain-in-the-neck-again kind of way.

She giggled. "Mom wants to know if you're still alive."

I almost dropped the phone. Her mom radar must be beep-beep-beeping again. That, and I'd forgotten to check in.

"I don't know. Hey, Packrat? Am I alive?" Molly giggled. I whispered into the phone, "No worries, squirt." Seeing the geocache box swing from Packrat's hand, I asked, "Can Mom talk yet?"

I heard Molly take a deep breath, and pulled the phone away from my ear just in time.

"*Mommmmmmm!*" she shrieked. "Can you talk?" Two seconds later, Molly was back. "Nope. She's got a line at the register. But she said don't forget Maxwell!"

"I'm on my way—"

"Aaaaaand Packrat's mom says Aunt Lucy is here. Hurry back."

To Packrat, I said, "Your aunt?"

He shrugged. "Not really an aunt. Like an aunt, I guess, 'cause Mom wants me to call her Aunt Lucy even though she's an old college friend of hers. Gonna stay a week with us in the trailer. I'm moving to my tent."

We walked in silence. Molly breathed into the phone. I could hear the *scritch-scratch* sounds of a pencil on paper. Packrat put out a hand to keep me from stepping on a pile of dead, crunchy leaves.

"So?" I finally said into the phone. "Are we done?"

She sighed. "Yeah. I guess."

I took pity on the kid. "I'll take a bike ride with you when I get home, but I can't paddle home and hold the phone too."

" 'Kay."

Dead silence again.

"Bye, Molly."

The second sigh came through the phone so big, I swear it moved my hair. "Bye, Cooper."

Cooper and Packrat: Mystery of the Eagle's Nest

The two of us quietly paddled home the long way, which meant going along the shoreline instead of cutting straight across Pine Lake. We hadn't talked about it first, but I think we were both feeling the same way.

We had to check on our eagles. And their triplets.

Triplet eaglets were rare. Really, really rare. It wasn't often that *two* survived to adulthood, never mind three! Usually, the nest gets too small as they grow, so one falls out. Other times, one eaglet gets picked on by the rest, sometimes dying, when the mom and dad don't bring enough food fast enough. All our campers were crazy obsessed over whether or not all three would live. Whenever a camper only spotted two baby heads peeking over the edge of the nest, they'd get everyone worried for days until someone else finally took a picture of all three as proof.

But the next time a camper reported only two, it'd start all over again.

"So ya think we can fool those guys if we run into them?" Packrat asked.

"Yeah. If we show them this box," I said. "They'll think it's a case of mistaken identity—that their box went missing—and they'll move on. After that, we'll turn them in."

"To who? Your parents?"

"I don't know. Maybe Warden Kate when she gets back. She'll know who to report it to. And she won't freak out at the fact that we were chased through the woods." The words *like my Mom would* hung between us, unsaid.

We were almost at the Wentworths' dock now. It felt kind of weird, knowing Mr. and Mrs. Wentworth would never again come out through their slamming screen door to wave hello and ask me about the loons or turtles, or their favorite, the herons. The Wentworths had decided they were too old to maintain the big lakeside house, and none of their kids wanted it. So they had moved into town and were selling the house.

My eyes glanced at the big red-and-white FOR SALE sign. It always made me wonder two things: One, can I still call it the Wentworths' place, if there are no more Wentworths living in it, and two: What would the new owners think about having nesting eagles next door? The thing I'd learned from last summer was that not everyone liked nature and wildlife the way Packrat, Roy, and I did.

Whoever bought the Went—the place had better like eagles as much as Mr. Wentworth did, because they were as close as two neighbors could get! Sometimes, one of the adults would even perch on the chimney of the house. And I knew from hanging out with Mr. Wentworth on his porch that those eaglets could get wicked noisy too. Especially when they were hungry!

Right now, they looked really hungry as they shrieked, brown heads bobbing up and down. We stopped paddling to pull out our binoculars for a better look. The nest was perched at the tip-top of a white pine that leaned slightly to the left. The nest was so huge, it hung over the rock wall into the yard. I guess you could say it was actually halfway on the Went—on the property. It was made of branches, twigs, grasses, and fluff, and Warden Kate said it weighed about seven hundred pounds! There was one long, light brown stick that had gotten hung up in such a way that it stuck straight out the left side of the nest about three feet.

Those eagles had added a ton of stuff to it this year, too. They were still adding to it! I guess they knew they'd need a bigger house to keep their third eaglet safe. It was so deep that when an adult eagle was sitting low inside it, you could only see the very top of its white head.

The eaglets used their beaks to pull themselves higher on the nest, almost to the edge. You could still see some of their gray down in spots, but mostly they were brown from head to toe. At about six weeks old, each eaglet was bigger than a raven. Bigger than a duck! All three turned to look in the same direction across the lake, and called out with a bunch of short, squeaky, high-pitched calls.

"Must be lunchtime," Packrat said, binoculars still at his eyes.

One of the parents flew in, gliding across the top of the water so we could see its reflection below. Then it soared to the top of the tree with a big flapping trout in its talons. Reaching the nest, the eagle seemed to hang in midair for a second, its wings outstretched so you could almost count each brown feather. It dropped the trout in the nest before gracefully lowering its wings, folding them, and landing on the nest's edge.

Two of the eaglets let loose *Feed-me-first-feed-me-first-I'm-dying-over-here* cries. The largest one pulled himself across the nest with his beak again until he was closer. The adult nudged the trout toward him. It pecked at it once, twice.

Packrat whispered, "Go on. Take a big bite!"

The eaglet looked up and cried along with the other two.

"Well, he tried," I said.

I swear that parent sighed before it dug into the trout, tearing it apart to feed the eaglets in no particular order. Every now and again, the eagle would raise its beak to gaze across the lake, off into the distance where its mate soared, looking for the next meal.

"How did the eagle in the box go from a life like that to having its head on a stick?" Packrat asked out loud. "Why would anyone *do* that?"

"I know what I'd do if I caught them!" I smacked a fist into my other hand.

"What would Warden Kate do?" Packrat asked.

I sat straight up. "Hey! You know, if those goons do stop in the campground, we can get their license-plate number and really good descriptions to pass on to her. Then she can figure out who the boss is, and maybe who really owns the stuff." And that, I thought to myself, was a plan any investigating warden would make.

Buuuuuut probably not a plan any mother would like. Especially my worrywart mom.

Chapter 4

The bald eagle has been a US national emblem since 1782, and a spiritual symbol for Native Americans for much longer than that.

With the geocache box tucked away in my backpack, we walked up from the lake to the camp office. As we passed the Snack Shack, Big Joe called out, "Your mom's looking for 'Maxwell.' Have you seen him?"

Packrat snorted.

I looked at my watch. Then started to jog. I was supposed to be working five minutes ago.

At the office, I found Mom in a panic. Once she saw me come through the door, her eyes went from nervous to smiley to serious and narrowed.

"Coop! Where have you been? I was worried sick you'd been hurt or gotten lost—"

"*Mom!* I wouldn't get lost on my own trail!" Wondering if the goons had come in yet, I asked, "Did a big—"

Mom's eyes were not on me. They were searching the store for little customers. She put a hand on my back to gently push me toward the back of it. "Hurry!" she said. "You've got to get in the suit."

"But—"

"If Maxwell Moose doesn't get out there soon, I'm going to have some angry parents on my hands."

I sighed. "I know, I know. The kids want the moose."

"Well, that too. But your father is out there now. Entertaining them." She pointed out the side window. Dad had a long, yellow balloon in his hands, twisting and twisting and twisting the neck of what would probably be a giraffe.

Pop! The whole thing blew up in the face of a big-eyed toddler.

Mom was right; I had to get out there. "But I've got to ask you something right after, okay?"

"I'm not going anywhere." Hearing another *pop,* she grimaced. "Unless I'm outside handing out free ice cream to crying kids."

Mom grabbed my backpack and slid it off my back. Taking one last look to be sure no one was watching, she pushed me into the storage room, tossing the backpack in after me. The decoy geocache box hit the floor with a clunk.

Packrat slid into the room to help, closing the door to guard it in case a curious kid tried to open it up. I flipped off my sneakers and opened the top of the stand-up freezer. Digging around the extra ice-cream-on-a-stick stuff, I found the ice-pack vest under a box of straw-berry sundae cups. I slid the vest on and sucked in a breath. Man, was it cold! Goose bumps formed on my neck. I knew it'd feel just right later on, though.

Packrat passed me the heavy, large, furry one-piece suit. I stepped into the legs and zipped up the front zipper just enough so the top half of it would hang on my waist for a minute. Next came the oversize, car-toonish, blue-and-white sneakers. Sneakers on a moose. I'd worn the suit for about a month now, and it still cracked me up every time I put them on.

Next, Packrat held Maxwell's head with both arms, the back of it facing me. This was the part I didn't like so much. It's a good thing I'm not claustrophobic, 'cause if I was, there'd be no way I'd put my head in it.

Two under-the-arm loop straps hung out from the opening at the bottom. Packrat tipped the gigantic head so the dark, gaping opening faced me. I put my arms through those loops first. Packrat helped lift it up, then lowered the humongous head over mine until it rested on my shoulders. It'd taken me a couple of weeks to get used to the weight of it, so I could move around without feeling like I was going to fall forward from the weight of the nose.

Inside, a smaller, helmet-like contraption went around my head. I put a hand up inside the opening by my left ear to find the helmet's chin strap, pulling it over to the other side and snapping it into place. Now I could pull the rest of the furry suit up to put my arms through the sleeves. Packrat finished zipping me all the way up, under my chin.

"Hands," he said.

I held out my left, and lifted my chin a bit so I could see out the round mesh hole underneath the mouth as Packrat slid the brown, furry mitten on my hand and tucked it into the sleeve. As we covered my right hand, he said, "Give me the usual signal when you're done."

"Okay," I said, my voice sounding muffled. "Hey, watch the little boy with the pirate-skull necklace and the plastic sword, wouldya? He kept trying to chop off my tail yesterday."

Packrat laughed. "Yep. I'm on it." He opened the door a crack. "Coast is clear, Maxwell."

I had to stand sideways and shuffle my feet to get the huge moose antlers through the storage-room door. Once we were in the store, I was under strict orders to walk in a straight line for the front door. The first time I'd worn the suit, I had gotten mobbed by kids. I'd turned left to see one, and an antler had taken out the postcard rack. Everything had crashed to the floor, postcards falling like snow. When I'd turned to see what all the noise was about, the other antler had taken out the key-chain rack. When I'd turned back around, I'd clocked my dad in the nose. The kids had thought it was all pretty funny. Mom had not. Ever since, Maxwell had met his little fans out in front of the building.

I stepped out of the office into the bright sunlight.

"Maxwell!"

"Max!"

"Look, Mommy! It's the moose!"

"Ooooooooooo. He's big."

I gave high fives to all the kids that wanted one. I rubbed heads, messing up hair. I posed for photos. Every now and then there was a kid who stood behind the crowd, watching carefully but not coming too close. Those were the ones I always tried hardest to win over, to make them laugh, or at least get them to give me a low five. I didn't mind that they were scared of me. I mean, think about it: Wouldn't you be scared, too, if you saw a wicked tall moose coming at you, standing on two legs, with huge green eyes? Wearing sneakers?

I hadn't been outside five minutes and I was already dripping, sweaty wet inside the suit, even with the ice-pack vest. I could usually go for twenty minutes—thirty, tops—before I started to feel a little wobbly-like-weird. Dehydrated, Mom called it.

Through two little round holes in the nose, I saw Roy sitting on the porch railing, talking to a blond-haired older kid I didn't know. I should say *Roy* was talking like crazy, arms waving, while the kid seemed kind of bored. He kept checking his phone. I looked at the little campers around me as I put a finger to my pretend mouth. In really exaggerated slow motion, I snuck up on Roy from behind. The little kids, and some big kids, too, started giggling. I thought the blond kid might warn him, but he just looked up from his phone, then back down again.

Roy didn't see me coming until I'd already rubbed his red hair with my furry paw, getting it to stand up on the top of his head. He jumped up and whirled on me, but there was a smile on his face too. "Maxwell! I'm gonna get you for that!" He hopped the railing to chase me around the campers, chairs, and planter poles, while I tried to hide behind trees and little kids and stuff.

Finally, it was photo time. One by one, each family placed their kid or kids around me. I'd do stuff like lean on their heads with my elbow, or put two fingers up behind them. Finally, the mom or dad would say, "Smile!" Of course, Max's face always had a smile, so I didn't really have to do anything. When a parent got bossy or mean to their kids about

the whole thing, I could stick my tongue out at them and they'd never even know.

Packrat was wrapping things up, telling the kids Maxwell had to go home for lunch, when I saw a guy coming out of the store. I couldn't see his face, but I saw a red tie.

Campers didn't wear ties.

I moved my head up, hoping I was wrong, thinking what I was thinking. As a big, square face filled the peek hole at the end of Maxwell's nose, I groaned quietly.

Red-tie guy. *Mikey.*

My mother was giving him directions. She pointed down the street and handed him a car pass to hang in his rearview mirror. He'd registered to stay!

I heard Packrat suck in a breath.

Mom smiled at the goon. She put a hand on his tree trunk of an arm and laughed at something he'd said.

I wanted to yell *Run! Run from the creepy goon, Mom!*, but Maxwell wasn't supposed to talk, never mind yell. I moved my head around and sure enough, there was Moose, the blue-tie guy. He was on the phone, and it looked like he was arguing with whoever was on the other end. I tapped Packrat on the shoulder and tipped my head toward Mikey. Then I made a motion for him to stay. Using my silly, hip-swinging Maxwell Moose walk, I went over and pushed myself between Mom and the goon. Maxwell Moose to the rescue!

"Maxwell!" Mom gave me a kiss on the nose before introducing me to the goon. "This is our campground mascot. Do you have any kids, Mr. Smith?"

Mr. Smith? *Reeeally?* She fell for that? Give me a break.

"No, I don't. My brother and I are here on business." Mikey nodded toward Moose. "Just for one night."

"Well, just let me know if you need anything," Mom offered. "Maxwell, is it time for you to go in now?"

I shook my head and she frowned. "Not too much longer, okay?"

I put my hands up in an okay-you're-the-boss pose. She leaned in close to whisper, "I don't want Maxwell fainting in front of the little ones."

I put my hands on either side of my head in an *Oh no!* kind of way. Mom laughed. She loved that look, and I knew it.

"Maaaaax-well!" a little girl called from behind me. Just the opportunity I needed. I made a motion to her mom like I was holding a camera. Did she want to take a picture?

"Sure!" the mom said. I did my high-five, hair-rubbing thing with the kid, all the while backing up slowly. I gave a thumbs-up sign with one hand, and put my other hand on her daughter's head, still trying to listen to the dumb goon on the phone.

"I'm sorry, boss, but . . . Yes, I know the buyer isn't going to pay all that money for toys and a logbook . . . Hey, now wait a minute." He threw up one hand in exasperation "It's not our fault! What are the chances there'd be another green, waterproof box out there in the woods? Woods no one lives in? We went back as soon as you called and said the buyer grabbed the wrong—"

The goon hung his head. He mumbled, "Yeah. I guess we shoulda secured the area before dropping the stuff off. Yeah, I guess we shoulda remembered the tracking device, too. But are you *sure* the buyer didn't take the parts? Maybe he's doin' a double-cross." Both goons cringed as a loud, angry voice came through the phone. "Sorry . . . sorry . . . sorry, boss. Not my place to question it. The buyer is usually right."

So eagle-parts thieves had their own kind of customer service?

The goons stood together now. I kept doing my goofy poses so the camper would keep taking pictures. Sweat ran down my face, dripping off my nose as I listened in.

"We've checked into the campground. Got a site with water, electric, sewer, and cable. Wireless, too! Okay, okay, right. Sorry. We aren't here on vacation," the goon said, relaying the boss's responses to his brother. "No. No. We didn't search for the kids yet, but you know, we didn't get a good look at them, so the chances are slim . . . It's not a big campground. It'll maybe take us a day to see if the box is here or not."

I smiled to myself inside the moose suit. This was gonna be easier than I thought; they'd already practically given up.

I turned to the little girl and made a big show of waving good-bye while peeking out the nose holes for one last look at the goons. Moose still had his ear to the phone. Suddenly, his whole body stood tall at attention. He gave his brother a panicky look. The kind of look Molly has on her face when she's been caught standing on a chair with her hand in the cookie jar.

"But . . . you've never . . . we've never . . . you're here *now?*"

Chapter 5

*When an eagle wants to warn another bird away from
its food, you may see it* mantling, *or hunkering over it,
wings outspread.*

I shuffled back over to Packrat, who stood with Roy. He was whispering to him, telling him about the goons, I could tell. I knocked him on the head a bunch of times.

"*Oww! Oww! Oww!*" He covered his head with his arms. "Okay! I get it!" He turned to the crowd and announced, "Looks like Maxwell's really got to go."

"Maxwell's gotta *peeeeee?*" said a little boy.

Packrat laughed. "That's a new one!"

Roy snickered and said to the little boy, "Yeah. Maxwell's gotta pee. C'mon, let's go find a potty, Max." Roy led the way through the crowd while Packrat followed behind, telling all the kids when and where I'd show up next, and basically trying to get them not to follow us.

I got out of that moose suit so fast, it was as if I really *did* need to pee. Even with Packrat helping to put the suit away, I felt like we were wasting precious time.

Packrat gave the secret knock to say I was changed out of the suit. Roy opened the door from the outside. "The coast is clear. So, what's going on? Eagle heads in boxes? Chased by fancy-dressed, shady-looking guys? The one time I don't go with you . . ."

"*Shhhhhh!*" Packrat and I said at the same time.

From the corner of my eye, I saw Mom checking in a short bald guy at the counter. Was that the boss? Or was it the tall, dark-haired, Native American guy talking on his phone in the trailer-supply section? The lady making coffee at the coffee bar? Or the tall, blond-haired guy shopping with the boy with the phone?

"No talking here," I said, closing the back-room door firmly.

Once we were at the far end of the porch, I looked back toward the goons who were still in the driveway and whispered, "This is top-secret stuff, Roy. I think we should just keep the parts hidden until these guys leave."

Mikey was still on the phone, leaning up against their motor home. Moose paced back and forth in front of him. He had such a puppy-dog-who'd-done-something-wrong look on his face, I knew they were still getting yelled at by their boss.

Roy and Packrat stared at them. "Hey! Don't you both stare at the same time!" I hissed. "They don't know who Packrat and I are."

Roy bent down to tie his shoe while looking back at them. "They're checking into the campground?"

I nodded. "Already did. They're on the phone with their boss. He's here somewhere, and it's freaking them out because they forgot to put a tracking device on the box."

Packrat's eyes got round. "*Here*-here? Or here, like, here in the neighborhood?"

I paused. They hadn't exactly said *here*-here. "I don't—I'm not sure."

Packrat picked up a candy wrapper from the ground and took it to the trash can at the other end of the porch. When he got back, he looked at me with even wider eyes. "Those guys are huge!"

"You can say that again."

Roy turned to stand by me, crossing his arms. He took another look at the goons. One side of his mouth curled upward. "They don't look so tough. We can take them."

Packrat and I smiled at each other and shook our heads. "We wait for them to leave," I said firmly, just in case Roy was serious. "Then we hand the box over to Warden Kate when she gets back. I don't want anyone to know we were chased through the woods, or that we have eagle parts."

I looked Roy in the eye. "Remember what Warden Kate said about how much trouble we could get into for having an eagle feather? Not to mention a whole eagle!"

"The fine is a hundred thousand dollars and some jail time," said a voice I didn't recognize. We all turned, and there was the kid who'd been talking to Roy on the porch and the guy in the store. He put his hands in his shorts pockets and rocked back on his heels. "Of course, it goes up from there, the more you have."

"Hey, Gavin!" Roy beamed. "I wondered where you went!"

I gave Packrat a what-the-heck look. How long had he been there? Packrat shrugged.

Mom came out of the store. In six long steps, she reached me, wrapped her arms around me, and gave me a great big bear hug.

I gasped, "*Mommmm!* You're choking me."

"I almost sent out the troops when I didn't hear from you."

"Mom!" *Sheesh.* Did she always have to do this in front of the guys? Roy's mom never worried about him like this.

She turned to Gavin. "It took forever for him to convince me to let him make a geocache trail. You know, since most of it is on the other side of the lake and all. What if he fell and broke his leg or something? It'd take forever to find him."

I looked toward Mikey and Moose, who were still talking to each other outside their motor home. Then I looked at Mom. If she only knew.

If she knew.

If she knew!

My mind whirled.

If she knew, I'd never be allowed to set foot on the other side of the lake again. It didn't matter that we'd gotten away from the goons and saved the eagle parts. Last summer, it'd taken a month after Mr. Bakeman had run me over with his boat for her to stop calling me on the radio every ten minutes when I was on the lake.

Oh no. She couldn't know. Not one thing.

"These are the kids you were talking about? *They* set up the geo-cache trail?" The kid's eyes narrowed as he looked between my friends and me. What? He didn't believe her?

Mom must've missed it, because she puffed up with pride as she threw a hand on both Packrat's and my shoulders. "I hoped you boys would meet Gavin! He and his dad, Mr. Valley, checked in yesterday, and when I found out he was an Eagle Scout—"

Again, Gavin butted in. "You, the two of you, made the entire trail? With the boards to cross the wet spots? And the coordinates list for the caches?" With each question, his voice got louder, carrying down the porch and into the driveway where the goons had just gotten off the phone and opened their motor-home door.

I cringed. Mom kept bragging, which I usually didn't mind, but now . . .

"The entire thing was their idea, and it's been a huge hit with the other kids, too. Cooper and Packrat—"

"And Roy," I added.

"And Roy," Mom smiled at him, as she took a hand from my shoulder to put it on his, "laid it out and marked it so you can boat over for a half-day hike, or leave from the back of the campground on foot for a full-day hike."

Gavin smiled, but there was something about his eyes that bothered me. They were clear and serious, taking everything in, reminding me of an eagle. Ever watchful. Waiting to pounce. On what, I had no idea. "Impressive," he said.

"Mom," I started, using my best you're-embarrassing-the-heck-out-of-me voice.

She kept talking. "The three of them keep a close eye on it, too—to make sure none of the caches go missing, or get taken by non-geocachers."

"My dad and I hiked the half trail yesterday afternoon," Gavin said quietly.

"You did?" Mom exclaimed. "I didn't realize."

"We were taking a break from hunting for antiques. Decided to try the trail and found all but one, the one called Stone Wall."

I sighed. That must be the one the buyer had grabbed by mistake. The stupid goons had hidden theirs in the wall too. It was all starting to make sense now. Kind of.

Packrat made eye contact with me, then looked over toward the motor home. The goons stood frozen, Mikey with one foot inside, Moose right behind him.

Gavin looked quickly at his phone, then said, "Some of your clues were kinda hard. But every cache was, like, wicked close to the coordinates you gave us."

I opened my mouth to interrupt him, but he kept going and going and going. What was he trying to do—get us noticed by the goons?

"My favorite was when you got that small box," Gavin's large hands moved to mime a small square, "to blend in so well with the side of the birch tree."

Mikey and his brother slowly turned to look our way.

"Camouflaging it with birch bark so it was hard to see, then putting the capsule inside it, with the teeny-tiny pencil and logbook, was genius."

I looked at Roy and Packrat. How could I make him stop?

The goons started walking our way.

"So!" I said quickly, while Gavin took a breath. "How about the fishing? Anyone get out on the lake today?"

Mom tipped her head to one side. "Cooper? What's gotten into you? You can usually talk for hours about this!"

A shadow slowly fell over my mom as the two goons walked up to tower behind her. Mikey looked over her head, his eyes focusing as they met mine, like a bobcat spying its prey. He reached out to grab Mom's shoulder. Packrat gasped. Roy moved closer to my mom.

The goon raised an eyebrow. "Geocaching trail? Hidden boxes and stuff? Tell us more!"

Chapter 6

When eagles attack, they swoop down at speeds of up to 100 miles an hour.

No way would Mom smile that big if she knew this same goon had just chased us through the woods a few hours ago. Just then, the dark-haired Native American guy I'd seen earlier in the trailer-supply section poked his head out the store door. "Joan, is your husband around? I have a problem with the water line on my motor home."

"He's not far away, Hawke. Let me call him on the radio for you." Mom patted the goon's hand before stepping away to walk down the porch to the door. She turned back once to add, "My son and his friends can tell you everything you want to know about the trail. Ask them anything. We have the hiking GPS for rent at the front desk that'll give you the coordinates for every geocache."

"Except one!" Gavin laughed at his own joke.

Mom was the only one who thought his joke was funny, her laugh trailing back to join his as she walked into the store.

Gavin checked his phone again. "My dad's waiting for me in the store. He's found another antiques shop to investigate. See you kids later."

And just like that, he was gone. That left the three of us alone with the goons. We stood shoulder to shoulder at the end of the porch, the railing behind us. They stood shoulder to shoulder between us and the rest of the porch.

They made the bigger wall.

"Hey, Mikey, guess what? I *can* pick them out of a lineup!" Moose broke the silence, pointing at Packrat and me. "Those two! Those are the ones that grabbed our stuff!"

Mikey elbowed his brother in the ribs. "Why don't you say it a little louder so the people at the pool can hear ya? Idiot."

"Hey!" Moose complained, rubbing his chest.

Mikey ignored him, eyeing me instead. "You have something that doesn't belong to you."

Roy crossed his arms and stared at Mikey coolly. "We do?"

I groaned under my breath. Packrat started going through his coat pockets, pulling stuff out left and right. "A fire starter? Nope, that's mine. Fishing tackle? Mine again. Dog leash? Hmmm . . . that might be yours."

Roy grinned and leaned toward me. In a whisper-that's-really-meant-to-be-heard voice, he said, "I'll bet you an ice cream Packrat doesn't have what he's looking for."

My friends were gonna get us killed!

I tried to smooth things over. I took a little step forward to stand in front of my friends. "Listen, we don't know what you're talking about. Or where it is."

Mikey's smirk disappeared. Scowling, he leaned in to whisper, "Listen yourself: I don't know about you," he pointed to Roy, "but you, and the one with the pockets, are the kids we saw in the woods. We want that box, and we want it now."

"You mean Cooper's geocache box?" asked Molly.

No, no, no, *no!* Where had *she* come from? I turned to look behind me, hoping the little sneak didn't actually have it. Seeing that she was holding an oversize lollipop and not the box, I let out the breath I'd been holding. *Whew!*

Mikey's big, square face softened as he looked down at her. His eyes still glinted, though, enough to keep me on edge. "Yes."

"Whyyyyy?" Molly licked her lollipop and turned from side to side.

"We want to see what one of those boxes looks like," he said. "For when we—" He looked to his brother for help.

"For when we go out to—" Moose looked back at his brother with his eyebrows raised.

"To . . ." Mikey waved one hand in the air, fishing for his words. "To . . . well . . . go out geo—looking for them."

"I know where one is! Hang on!" Molly turned and skipped down the porch and into the store before I could blink.

A group of kids walked by with towels on their arms. "Hey, Coop! Guys! We're hanging out at the lake. Come down!"

I waved to show them I'd heard. The five of us held our ground, standing in our spots. Watching each other.

An older couple leaned over the railing to ask where the rec hall was. Packrat answered them. A family of two adults and two little kids rode by on their bikes. Still another family walked their dog while voting on where they'd go sightseeing next. Two teens bounced a basketball as they talked about a girl they'd met the day before.

Still, we stood. Waiting.

Packrat reached behind me to poke me in the back. I knew what he was asking. Did I want him to go distract Molly?

I shook my head. Trying to pretend it wasn't us in the woods obviously wasn't going to work. These guys wouldn't budge until I gave them proof. And I wasn't gonna let them have those eagle parts.

Time to use the decoy.

Molly came back, carrying the box by its handle. All the while, she smiled up at me like she'd discovered a new species of bird. "You left it in your backpack in *Maxwell's* room." She gave me a big, dramatic wink. She thought she was such a big kid now that she knew giant stuffed animals who walked on two legs weren't really real.

Roy reached out for the box. I took it first. If they were going to come after someone, it should be me.

Mikey surprised me by crouching down to Molly's level. His face broke out into a wide smile. "Aren't you a clever little thing?"

You've got to be kidding me. I expected this from regular campers, but bad-guy-type goons? Little did they know Molly could get them to empty their pockets for her in a heartbeat if she wanted to. And she always managed to figure out the one thing you were hiding. Like the geocache box zipped up tight in my backpack.

Mikey hooked a thumb my way. "Is this your brother?"

Molly, the traitor, giggled and nodded.

"Well, he ought to thank you for finding it for him." Mikey patted her on the head as he stood. "What if someone had stolen it? Wouldn't he feel horrible? Now why don't you run along, so I can talk to your brother for a bit."

Molly skipped off the porch, across the campground entrance, and up the sidewalk to our house. Mikey slowly stood to watch her go. "Cute kid," he said, scratching his chin. "You must have to watch her real close in a big place like this."

Message received. I had two choices. One: I could keep trying to convince these guys we had no clue where their eagle parts were, and hope they left; or two: I could tell them where I'd hidden the real box of parts and know for sure they would never bother Molly, my friends, or me again.

"Open the box!" Mikey said.

I looked toward the house and hesitated.

"Excuse me." A lady's voice came from behind the goons. Mikey and Moose jumped, then parted. A short, blonde woman stood with her hands on her hips. She stared up at one goon, then the other. "Everything okay over here?"

Packrat breathed a sigh of relief. "It's fine *now*." Looking at me, he added, "This is the lady I told you about. My mom's old friend, Lucy."

"Who're you calling old?" Lucy teased. She ruffled his hair. "How'd you know who I was?"

"Mom showed me a picture from your college yearbook."

Lucy grinned. "You look just like her, you know." Her fond smile for Packrat disappeared as she turned to the two goons. "From over there, it kind of looked like you were harassing these kids."

If I hadn't been so scared, it would have been funny, the way this little woman could make the two big guys fidget.

Moose burst out, "But, they've got—"

Mikey elbowed him. "We didn't mean anything. They just seem to have picked up something of ours—by accident—and we were asking them about it."

Lucy looked at Packrat. "Is that true?"

Packrat nodded.

She pointed to the geocache box I held. "Is that it?"

We all nodded this time.

"Is it theirs?" She hooked her thumb back at the goons.

They nodded like bobbleheads.

We shook our heads, signaling *No*.

"They think it is—" began Packrat.

"But it really isn't—" Roy said.

"We were checking the caches on the geocache trail when we found *this* box." I quickly held it out. "But it's ours."

Lucy sighed. "You know, whenever my suitcases get mixed up with someone else's, there's only one way to figure out whose is whose. Open it up."

"That might not be such a good idea," said Mikey.

"Are you sure you want to see?" said Moose, who got another elbow from Mikey.

"You two are acting more like kids than these guys are." She tipped her head our way.

Maybe I felt a little braver with Lucy right there, but I couldn't resist messing with them a bit. These guys still thought it was theirs—and they didn't want Lucy to see what was in it. Looking Mikey right in the eye, I said, "I have no problem opening it up."

Mikey scowled at me. Lucy gently said, "Go ahead."

The goons actually looked nervous. I took my time, slowly setting the box on the porch, then pausing to glance at Moose. I flipped the clasp on the right, and looked at Mikey. This might have been a bit too much, since Mikey clenched his fists.

"Wait!" cried Moose, putting a hand on the box.

"What on earth is wrong with you all?" Lucy said. "Just open the box so we can see who it belongs to."

I lifted the lid ever so slowly. Packrat reached around me to pull out a McDonald's rubber ducky. He held it up and squeezed it once, twice.

Roy grabbed the logbook and waved it toward Mikey. "See?"

Packrat squeaked the duck twice more. "Ours."

Lucy tipped her head to one side to look up at the goons. "Problem solved."

"But we saw—" Moose said.

Lucy put her hands on her hips again. "You saw what?"

"We made a mistake," Mikey said, grabbing his brother's sleeve. "C'mon, Moose."

"But—"

"C'mon!" Mikey let go of the sleeve to grab Moose's tie and tug him back toward the motor home.

"Wait a minute," Lucy called.

I froze. Packrat stopped squeaking the duck. Roy stopped smiling. What had she seen? Why'd she call them back?

Mikey turned with a hopeful look on his face.

"I think you two owe these kids an apology," Lucy explained.

I tried not to smile, but failed as the goons mumbled their *I'm sorry*'s before scrambling back to their motor home.

We'd done it. We had convinced them that we didn't have their stuff.

With any kind of luck, they'd go home tomorrow. I'd take the stash to Warden Kate when she got back.

Mom never had to know a thing.

Chapter 7

Female eagles do most of the egg-sitting, making sure the eggs stay at 99.5 degrees Fahrenheit. The male will take his turn so his mate can stretch, fly, and feed.

The next day was a workday. I signed in on my time card at seven a.m., and after stopping by the Snack Shack for a bagel, I headed over to the men's and ladies' bathrooms. At this time of day I didn't have to do a full clean—just a wipe-the-sinks-and-sweep-the-floor-and-stock-the-toilet-paper kind of clean. I had to be quick, too, because sleepy campers who've just rolled out of their sleeping bags don't like seeing a CLOSED FOR CLEANING sign on the bathroom door.

Afterward, I made a beeline for the office. Grabbing a juice from the cooler, I went up behind Mom to peek over her shoulder.

"How were the bathrooms?" she asked, without turning around. She was looking at the checkout list.

And so was I.

"Fine," I said. *The goons weren't on it.*

"Pool next?"

"On my way."

As I went out the door, Hawke came in. I stood aside so he could pass, and he smiled down at me.

"Coffee on?" he asked my mom.

"Always," she replied.

I turned to leave, but had to step aside again. Gavin walked right by me, followed by his dad, who said, "Mornin'!"

"Morning," I replied, before I realized Mr. Valley was waving at Hawke across the store. "Just the man I wanted to see," he called out, then went to join him. "I hear you've been out and about the area already, and I wanted to pick your brain."

Gavin leaned against the coffee counter, listening to the two men. He glanced over at me and then away again, like I wasn't even standing there.

Without looking up from her paperwork, Mom said, "Cooper! Pool." Whatever.

If I had a choice between vac-ing the pool and cleaning bathrooms, I'd choose the pool every time. But it's sooooo boring! I'm surprised I've never fallen asleep and fallen face-first in the water. I have Roy and Packrat to thank for that, because one (or both) usually keeps me company, hanging over the fence and chatting.

But today, Roy was on duty too. He'd won the cooler job of splitting wood on the log splitter with Dad by shooting paper over my rock.

"They leave yet?" Roy asked over the radio for the seventeenth time that morning.

"Not yet," I told him.

Packrat had been dragged to the mall by his mom and Lucy. He'd called me on the radio to say he was gonna try to play sick, but honestly, I knew it wouldn't work. His mom had pulled the we-have-company-so-be-nice card. I grinned, thinking about the one time he'd twisted my arm into going shopping with him and his mom. She'd insisted on walking into a pink store that had nothing but ladies' stuff in it. She'd also insisted we follow her, 'cause she was only going to be a minute.

So Packrat and I had covered our eyes with our hands. We'd run right into a dummy display, knocking it to the floor and sending bright-colored underwear flying everywhere. His mother was so embarrassed, she'd pulled us out of there and didn't talk to us all the way home.

"Hey! Whatcha doin'?" Gavin's voice brought me back to the edge of the pool.

I looked at the vacuum and then to Gavin with a raised eyebrow. It was not very customer-servicey of me, I know. But really! He'd barely looked at me ten minutes ago. And besides, it was a stupid question.

"Is it fun?" He rested his arms on top of the chain-link fence and leaned way over to see the vacuum in the water.

I stopped vacuuming. What was going on? Why was he being so weirdly friendly now? My mouth opened, a rude comment on the tip of my tongue, but then I had a better idea.

"Yeah! It's my favorite job." I looked around like I wasn't supposed to do what I was about to do. Which, technically, I wasn't. "You wanna try?"

"Okay."

I waited, trying not to give away how surprised I was that he'd taken the bait, while he jogged around the pool and through the gate to me. I showed him how to push the broom back and forth slowly, with straight rows, so he'd catch every single hair, flake of skin, and pine needle that had settled to the bottom of the pool overnight.

"Slow is the secret," I said, "so you don't push everything back up to float around in the water again."

Once he'd gotten the hang of it, I pulled the cover off the square skimmer hole in the pool deck. Swimming inside the skimmer were three yellow-eyed green frogs.

I knelt down on the concrete and, after four tries, managed to catch one in my cupped hands.

"I have a great place for you," I whispered to the frog as it tried to squeeze its slippery body between my fingers. "You need freshwater, not this chlorinated stuff." I glanced back at Gavin, to make sure he hadn't heard me. Being a bigger kid, he'd probably laugh to hear me talking to frogs.

I took it to Mom's garden and let it go on the rocks next to the pond. Quick as a flash, it jumped into the pond, then poked its nose out of the water to look up at me.

"You're welcome," I said. To Oscar, my three-legged pet frog, I added, "Play nice."

After transferring the other two frogs, the last one being really tricky to catch, I emptied the skimmer of all the pine needles it had sucked in overnight. Then I straightened all the pool chairs and emptied the trash cans.

"Hey," I called across the pool to Gavin. "I'm gonna get the water-testing kit."

He looked up and smiled at me. "I got this. Go ahead."

Still weird.

I went behind the store counter to get another Maxwell Moose pen from the drawer to write the test results. I glanced at the checkout list again. Those goons still hadn't left.

At the edge of the pool, I sat cross-legged with a clipboard and my pen, and opened the test-kit box. Holding up the plastic tube tester full of pool water, I put three drops of a clear solution into it. I swirled the water a little, held it up, and watched as the water turned light pink. According to the chart on the tube, Dad was going to need to add a little bit of chlorine to the pool.

"So, hey, like, what were you guys talking about yesterday—having eagle parts?" Gavin said across the pool. "You know that's illegal, right?"

The tester I held in my hand flew into the air, bright-pink-tinted water fell onto my paperwork, and the tester bounced off the pool deck to land in the water. I leaned over to scoop it out before it could sink to the bottom.

"They aren't ours!" I snapped. So he *had* heard us! But how much? And what did he care?

Gavin glanced up at me. "So they're someone else's. Are you hold-ing them for—"

I must've had a mad look on my face, 'cause he gave me an *I'm sorry* look. "Okay. Don't tell me. But did you know only Native Ameri-cans can own eagle parts?"

"Yeah," I said, immediately thinking of how I'd seen Hawke talking on his phone in the store yesterday.

"And did you know, even *they* buy pieces on the black market because they have to wait years to receive parts, too? And sometimes they need them in a hurry for their ceremonies?"

That, I didn't know.

Why didn't I know—and how did *he* know?

"Done," Gavin said. He leaned the vacuum handle against the pool side and turned to me.

"Thanks," I said.

He shrugged. "You're welcome." Then he checked his phone, walked out the gate, and off into the campground.

Weird.

Chapter 8

Using the air currents, eagles can reach heights of up to 10,000 feet and soar for hours. Their hollow bones help keep them aloft.

I inspected the pool floor after Gavin had walked out the gate. Not bad. Sparkly blue and ready. And just in time, too, as a line of sunbathers, toddlers with swimmies on their arms, and parents slathering their kids head to toe in sunscreen had formed on the other side of the gate. Ignoring the dad who checked his watch twice, then tried to catch my eye, I pulled the vacuum up and out of the water. I disconnected the hose and coiled it before hanging both the hose and the vacuum in their storage spots in the pump house.

As I opened the pool gate, a little girl giggled and pointed to the RULES sign hanging on the chain-link fence. "Look, Mom! It says 'No moose allowed in the pool'."

The mom winked at me. "Guess we'd better keep an eye out to make sure Maxwell doesn't try to sneak in," she said.

The girl frowned. "He goes on the hayride, right? I want to sit next to him."

This girl must have known the rec schedule by heart, because right then, Dad pulled up in the dump truck with our red, yellow, and green hay wagon behind it. "He can," I told her. "Just don't let him drive the truck." I heard her giggling again as I shut the gate behind me and headed in the store to change.

After playing a truck-stealing Maxwell for the campers on the hayride, then eating an early lunch, I grabbed my rake, shovel, trash bucket, and hand brush and threw them into the back of the golf cart.

Mom handed me a copy of her camper checkout list so I could use it to clean sites. I scanned it quickly. Those goons still weren't on it.

What the heck? This could only mean two things. One: They were going to be the kind of camper who leaves right at checkout time, not a minute early or a minute late. Or two: They weren't gonna leave at all.

"Hey, Mom? Call me if you have any more checkouts, okay?"

"I always do, Cooper."

I drove out to my first site and got started.

Cleaning sites was at the top of my favorite-maintenance-jobs list. I always got to wear my earbuds so I could listen to music while I raked the site to gather up any small bits of trash, cigarette butts, and leaves. Then I walked around its edges, checking for trash in the woods. I didn't rake there because if you took away the ground cover, the rain would run off onto the campsite and make puddles. Last, I brushed pine needles and leaves off the picnic table.

Normally, I could zone out and be in my own little world. But after I realized today was a quiet camping Tuesday in the middle of June, and this road was dead empty, I found myself looking over my shoulder a thousand times. After a while I took the earbuds out and tried to laugh at myself for being so paranoid. It wasn't as if the goons were gonna drive up, stuff me in their motor home, and drive off without anyone knowing.

Right?

Last night, Packrat, Roy, and I had celebrated fooling those goons. We were so sure they'd pull out today, and take their boss and buyer with them. I, for one, would feel better when the taillights of their motor home were on the other side of our gate.

I stood with one foot on the picnic table seat and the clipboard on my knee, crossing sites 20, 24, 25, and 26 off my list, when suddenly, arms wrapped around my neck. I staggered backwards. Legs wrapped around my waist. I staggered forward. I tried to turn and see who it was, but they put their hands over my eyes. "Hey!" I yelled. "Help!"

Reaching out with both hands, I tried to get a hold on a foot, a leg, a shirt, anything! Instead, I turned around in circles. Finally, I managed to grab a knee, hard. Two things popped into my head at the same time.

One: This was a little knee. A bony knee. Not a big-goon knee.

Two: There were giggles in my ear.

Molly.

"Don't do that!" I pulled her around to my front and dropped her on her feet.

Her eyes sparkled with laughter. "I got you!"

"Yeah, yeah, you got me." But only because I'd spooked *myself* by thinking about those goons. "Whatcha doing out here? Does Mom know where you are?"

"She told me I could come and get you if I came straight here and—" she paused, "—went straight back." Doing her best Mom impression—hands on hips, foot tapping on the ground—she said, "That Cooper! Always turning down his radio! How'm I s'posed to get him in an a-mergency?"

It must be important if Mom let Molly come get me. I pointed to the golf cart for her to climb in while I put the rake, shovel, and trash bucket into the back. "So, what's the big emergency?"

Molly shrugged her shoulders. "I dunno. Those two big guys came in—"

"What? Why didn't you say so sooner!" I jumped in the front seat. "Is she okay? Did they hurt her?" Turning the key, I put my foot on the gas pedal. "Hang on!"

Wide-eyed and gripping the side bar as we took off, Molly stared at me. "Cooper! What?"

I flew over a pothole, my head hitting the roof, Molly's butt coming off the seat. "You said the goons were bothering Mom."

She frowned. "No, I didn't. They just want the PGS stuff."

I slammed on the brakes. "Mom's okay? Wait, they want the GPS?"

Molly's eyes grew wider. She whispered, "Are they bad?"

I really, really thought about telling her the truth. I wanted to at least warn her not to go anywhere with them. Then I remembered what loose lips she had.

Pressing the gas pedal a little more gently this time, I carefully answered, "Nah. I just . . . umm . . . I didn't think they'd stay this long, and . . . umm . . . I thought they might give her a hard time about having to change sites." That had to be the lamest answer ever, especially with the campground half empty. They could've had ten sites if they wanted them.

"Mom got them a whole week. She's holding next week, too—in case they can't find what they're looking for." Molly had her fishing-for-more-information look on. "I like them. They always say hi. And they gave me a *biiiiiig* lollipop yesterday."

I slammed on the brakes again. Molly squealed.

"Are you crazy?" I wanted to shake that smile off her face. "Taking candy from str—"

"They asked Mom first!" she blurted. "I know the rules! You can ask."

I would. But for now I decided to pick her brain a little. Molly hung out in the office. A lot. She was smart for five. Smart enough to watch everybody, and everything they did, like a hawk. Mom forgot she was there a lot of the time.

Putting the cart in drive, I tried to sound like I couldn't have cared less when I asked, "So, what are they looking for?"

Molly looked at me funny. "Your boxes."

Well, duh. "They didn't talk about anything else? Like, maybe, beavers or loons or, I don't know, eagles?"

"Nope. They told Mom they want to find the lost box, though. The one Gavin and his dad didn't find."

I pulled alongside the office porch and jumped off the cart before it had come to a complete stop. Inside, I found Mom chatting with the goons. The geocache GPS lay on the reservations counter between them, and the list of coordinates to every cache was in Mikey's hand.

"Thanks for coming back," Mom said to me. She pointed to the GPS, then tucked a lock of hair behind her ear with a sigh. "I can't get this thing going, and these gentlemen would like to head out on your trail."

"But it's after lunch," I stalled, needing time to think. "You can't do the whole trail in half a day."

Mikey raised an eyebrow. "It doesn't get dark until eight."

"What if you get lost—or twist an ankle? Then it'd get dark fast and the trail markers would be hard to see." I used Mom's own words to me, on them. "Tell him, Mom. You don't rent the stuff after dark."

Mom gave me her will-you-let-me-handle-this look. "If we get this GPS stuff figured out in the next couple of minutes, they should be back just after dusk."

I picked up the GPS and turned it on. "Don't call us when you can't see the markers 'cause it's dark out."

"Cooper!" Mom said sharply.

"I'll consider myself warned," Mikey drawled.

I pushed buttons, refusing to meet Mikey or Moose's triumphant looks. I heard the front door open and close a few times. Hawke got in line behind Mikey and Moose, followed by another customer.

"I just don't know what to make of it," Mom said. "We've only had it a couple of months or so. I'm so bad with the whole technology thing."

My finger hesitated over the GPS, as I listened in.

"Always getting myself in a jam, and Cooper having to get me out of it. Even Molly knows how to run television remotes better . . ."

That was it! I tuned out Mom and turned just enough so no one could see the series of buttons I was about to hit. Taking a deep breath, I turned back to the counter, frowned at the GPS, and shook my head.

"I know why it's not working."

All eyes turned toward me, including Hawke's thoughtful ones from behind Moose.

"Somehow you deleted the coordinates, Mom." I sighed heavily, trying with everything I had to keep my smile inside.

"All of them?" she cried.

"Yep. All of them." I waited for her to give the big lugs the bad news, and she didn't disappoint me. Mom never, ever, ever messes with the safety rules.

"Well, that's it then," she said. When Mikey and Moose tried to talk over her, Mom put up a hand and stared them down. Which was kind of funny, since she had to look up to do it.

"It'll take Cooper at least an hour to enter all the coordinates one by one, and now there's no way you can make it back before dark. I can't let you—"

"I don't mean to interrupt," said Hawke, "but I believe your trail and geocache coordinates are online as well?"

"Yes, they are!" Mom said.

"Well, then, these gentlemen could access the coordinates using their phones and a GPS app."

For a couple of seconds, there was silence. Mikey looked at me, a smile slowly forming. "You don't say?" he said.

Chapter 9

If you were to count every feather on an eagle, you'd find about seven thousand.

"Knock, knock," I called. Without waiting for an answer, I pulled up Packrat's tent zipper and tossed my rolled-up sleeping bag inside.

"Hey!" Roy yelled.

I tossed the pillow in after it. When I bent at the waist to enter headfirst, both the pillow and the sleeping bag came back to hit me, plus a couple more.

Laughing, I plopped down on the tent floor, zipping the tent flap closed behind me.

One lantern lit the inside of the tent, but not all the way into the corners. Packrat and Roy sat cross-legged on their sleeping bags, looking at me expectantly.

"So, did ya bring 'em?" Packrat whispered.

From the middle of my rolled-up sleeping bag, I pulled out nine photos. Packrat had uploaded them from his camera onto my laptop, and I'd snuck into the campground office and used Mom's printer to print them out. Roy turned up the lantern. I laid the pictures out side by side in front of us. Four pictures of the dead eagle head on the carved stick, one from every side, and one with it in my hand. Two of the pile of loose feathers. One close-up of a single feather. Two of the yellow claw—one with it next to my hand to show how big it was.

"*These* were in that geocache box?" Roy's eyes darted back and forth between the photos. "You've got to be kidding me!"

I knew exactly what he meant. I still didn't get it myself. *Why?* Why would someone stash them in the woods, and use all this cloak-and-dagger, watch-your-back stuff to own them? It didn't make any sense.

"That's why I called you guys!" Packrat pulled a tablet out of his coat pocket. "You won't believe—"

Footsteps! All three of us froze in place, me with one hand above the photos, ready to sweep them under a pillow. The steps came closer and closer. Closer still. Two sets. They stopped on the dirt road right outside Packrat's campsite. They were so close, I could hear breathing from the bodies attached to those footsteps.

"I think we go left," said a woman's voice.

"The bathrooms are to the right," a man replied. "Honestly, you'd get lost in a paper bag."

I heard a light arm slap as the woman giggled and the footsteps moved away. We all breathed a sigh of relief so deep, I'm surprised the tent didn't lift off the ground from all the hot air.

Packrat started again. "You won't believe what I found online!"

I moved over to sit on Roy's sleeping bag so I could watch as Pack-rat, whose face was lit by the glow of the tablet, went into his bookmarks to pull up the website he'd found. Sliding the tablet across the tent floor to me, he asked, "Did you have any idea there was a place like this?"

The website page belonged to US Fish and Wildlife. It was all about something called an Eagle Repository. It explained that eagles are protected in the United States because they're our national symbol, so when they died—whether they were killed or died of old age, whether they were golden or bald—according to the law, they had to be sent there. Native Americans who wanted eagle parts for religious reasons could apply for them by filling out a request. No one else was allowed to own them.

"What are Mikey and Moose doing with them, then?" Roy said. "They aren't Native Americans."

"We don't know that for sure," Packrat replied. "Maybe their boss is."

"Check out the part where it says there's like a three-and-a-half-year wait for a whole eagle," I said, still reading. "If someone asks for just a wing or a claw or a feather, it's less time."

And I thought waiting for Christmas every year was bad.

Headlights hit the tent. We all froze. The car went past very slowly, but it did keep going.

Another sigh of relief rang through the tent.

"So the goons went out on the trail?" Roy asked, while Packrat took the tablet back, his fingers flying across the keypad to pull up another website.

I looked at him and nodded. "I was soooo close to keeping them off it. Then Hawke mentioned how your phone can be a GPS, and those goons took off. I hoped they'd get lost or a bear would eat them or something. But no, they came back."

"They didn't find the box, did they?"

Cooper and Packrat: Mystery of the Eagle's Nest

"Nah, there's no way they can get at it. Far as I can tell, they still think theirs is lost in the woods somewhere—"

"Umm, Coop?" Packrat's hands shook a little as he passed the tablet to me. "I know you're hoping those guys are gonna give up and leave without their stuff, but I don't think that's gonna happen." Packrat pointed halfway down the page.

"What are you waiting for? Read it!" Roy said to me.

"A single golden eagle feather can sell on the black market for as much as a hundred and fifty dollars," I read aloud. My head snapped up to meet Roy and Packrat's eyes. "Black market?"

"*Shhhhhh!*" Packrat said. "Not so loud."

Whispering now, I read,

> *Whole eagles can sell for $1,200. When this reporter asked an employee of the Eagle Repository why there was a black market for eagle parts, she replied, "Mostly, Native Americans acquire them legally. But with 3,000 names on the waiting list and only 1,000 eagles processed each year, it can take a very long time, so some people get impatient and turn to the black market for a quicker turnaround. Of course, there are always those buyers who aren't Native American. It's illegal for them to own eagle parts, but they want them for art, or just the thrill of owning them, so the black market is their only outlet."*
>
> *I next asked how eagle parts are used.*

Some part of me knew that headlights had hit the tent again, but . . . *Black market? Buyers? Eagles?* I kept reading aloud in a whisper.

> *"Whole eagles and their parts are used in a variety of ways," the employee replied, "for Native American religious*

*reasons such as dances, artwork, and traditional dress such as
a headdress. There are dance contests, too; the more realistic
the traditional dress, the more points that are given." She
showed this reporter an eagle head on a stick.*

I grabbed our photo off the tent floor and held it up to the computer screen to compare. Their sample had a golden eagle head on an
uncarved stick. Not the one we'd found, but close.

Suddenly, Packrat sucked in a breath. The tent zipper was being
raised! Roy and Packrat swept the photos under the nearest sleeping bag.

Packrat whispered, "The tablet!"

I hit a button and the screen blacked out. Scanning the tent floor, I
saw the corner of the eagle-claw photo poking out from under Packrat's
sleeping bag. I started to reach for it, but stopped when Packrat's mom
poked her head inside. She smiled at each one of us.

"Hey, just wanted you to know that we're back."

"Okay. We're good." Packrat made a go-away-what-the-heck-are-
you-doing-in-our-space motion with his hands.

His mom laughed. "Okay, I get it. This is a no-adult zone tonight."
Her head left the tent-flap opening.

I started to reach across for the photo again when Lucy's head
appeared. She scanned the inside much the same way Packrat's mom
had. "How are you guys doing?"

We all said, "Gooooood."

Lucy looked back over her shoulder, and to Packrat's mom, she
called, "If you're putting on coffee, Stacey, I'd love some."

What the heck? I mouthed to Packrat. He rolled his eyes.

As they heard Packrat's camper door close, Lucy turned back to us
and asked, "Are you all okay after yesterday's misunderstanding?" We
nodded quickly. She stared intently at me. "No more trouble from them?"
We shook our heads. I tried really, really hard to keep my eyes on her.

Don't look at the photo. Don't look at the photo.

"Okay, then. Just wanted to be sure. I'll leave you alone now," she said, backing out of the tent. We stared at the flap zipper as Lucy began to pull it down. Halfway down, for just a second, I could almost swear the zipping stopped. Then it jiggled a bit and I breathed a sigh of relief. It'd only been stuck. Finally, Lucy brought it all the way to the tent floor. "See you all tomorrow," she called to us.

Packrat and Roy started to bring the photos back out, but I stopped them. Pushing the claw photo further under the sleeping bag, I said, "Leave them, just in case they come back with cookies or something."

Roy glanced longingly toward the camper. His stomach rumbled.

"Here." Packrat fished around an outside pocket, pulled out a snack-pack of chocolate chip cookies, and tossed it to Roy. "Read the rest," he said to me. "You haven't gotten to the good part."

I turned the tablet back on, scrolling till I found where I'd stopped, and read on: "She showed this reporter an eagle head on a stick. I asked how much money a finished piece of artwork with eagle parts might be worth. 'Some artwork is worth half a million dollars,' the employee replied."

I dropped the tablet on my sleeping bag. "Half a million dollars?" I hissed.

"*Shhhhhh!*" Packrat and Roy said.

"Half a million?" I whispered this time, pulling out the photo of the eagle head on the carved stick.

Packrat's head bobbed up and down. "Yeah, I know! Right?"

We all fell silent. Packrat was right. Those goons weren't going anywhere. Not with that much money at stake.

Chapter 10

When an eagle catches a fish too heavy to lift out of the water, it might use its wings like oars to swim to shore, rather than let the fish go.

We were up long past midnight, talking about the mess we'd walked into. There was no way even my worrywart Mom could have dreamed up all this trouble. Scary eagle-parts traders show up looking for their illegal stash, just as we're checking our toy-holding geocache boxes?

Really?

There were three things I remembered from right before I fell asleep. Light rain *tap-tap-tapping* on the tent; Packrat's snores; and saying to Roy, "If Mom finds out, she'll never let me out of the campground again."

Packrat's screeching *ant-ant-ant-ant-ant* alarm went off at about seven. Packrat had been able to sleep through every alarm his mother had ever given him. The little travel alarm was extra annoying, but after a full minute, we figured he was gonna sleep right through this one too.

I put my hands over my ears. "Ahhh! Make it stop!"

Roy crawled halfway out of his sleeping bag to shove the lump that was Packrat. "Hey! C'mon! Shut that off!"

We heard muffled groans, something that sounded like *Hugh goat it. Tom left, inside parrot,* then more snores.

Roy and I looked at each other and laughed. I slid my arms from my warm sleeping bag to grab Packrat's coat. I reached into the top-left inside pocket to pull out the travel alarm clock and started to hit the off button, but then had a better idea.

I tapped the snooze button, opened the top of Packrat's sleeping bag, and threw the clock in.

Roy and I gave each other a high five, then laid back with our arms behind our heads. This was as good a time as any to figure something out.

"So what's up with this Gavin kid?" I asked.

Roy turned his head my way, his eyes asking a thousand questions that didn't come out of his mouth. "He's okay. Likes nature as much as you. As much as us. He's an Eagle Scout, so that makes him, like, a senior. He and his dad buy antiques and resell them for money. That's all I know. Why?"

I didn't know how, or even *if*, I should explain them, but I knew two things: One, I didn't trust Gavin. Something wasn't right—the way he hadn't paid any attention to us at first, and now was trying to be all helpful and stuff. Two, he rubbed me the wrong way. He hadn't really done anything—yet—so I went with the one thing I knew Roy couldn't stand. "He heard too much. I'm afraid he'll tattle on us or something. He was all weird at the pool yesterday."

Roy seemed to consider it. "Nah. He's okay. Besides, we were talking yesterday, and he knows a lot of nature and eagle facts. He can help."

"What?" I sat up. "You talked to him? About *the parts?*"

"What's the big deal?" Roy sat up too. His eyes got hard. "I'm no dummy. I didn't give him any information he didn't already have."

"Just don't tell him about the pics, okay?" I warned. "If those goons do find the stash, those photos are our only proof that there were any parts at all."

Roy's smile returned. "No worries. Hey, you never said exactly where you hid the box. I mean, I know it's in our canyon—"

Ant-ant-ant-ant-ANT. Packrat's sleeping bag practically left the floor when the alarm went off. He rolled back and forth, arms and legs pushing the bag all over the place, until his hand popped out of the bag's opening to toss the blaring alarm clock back at us.

Packrat's head popped out next. "That was mean," he said, sitting up to run a hand over his static-filled hair. "Really mean."

I smiled and shut the alarm off. Roy was snorting, he was laughing so hard. He pointed a shaky finger Packrat's way. "You shoulda . . . shoulda . . . seen . . ."

As we crawled out of our bags, my hand landed on the eagle photos. I grabbed them and arranged them into a pile. Packrat squinted at me. Yawning behind his hand first, he asked, "Want me to hide those in a pocket?"

I hesitated, then shook my head. "I got 'em."

Roy unzipped the tent. Cold, damp morning air rushed in. I pulled a plain blue sweatshirt over my head and tucked the photos in my back jeans pocket. Packrat pushed his arms through the sleeves of his coat, but Roy, he crawled through the opening in only his T-shirt.

"Aren't you cold?" I asked, stepping out behind him.

"Are you kidding?" he said, his red hair already damp from the drizzle. "This is shorts weather!"

The three of us went to the back door of the Snack Shack for our before-work breakfasts. The new deal with my parents, ever since Roy and Packrat got jobs here too, was that on the days we worked, we got a meal from Big Joe. I asked him for my usual hot chocolate with extra milk, and a toasted raisin bagel with cream cheese. Roy had two bacon, egg, and cheese sandwiches. Packrat asked for an extra-large, extra-chocolatey, hot cocoa.

"That's it?" Roy had already eaten one of his sandwiches and was unwrapping the second.

Packrat cupped his cocoa with both hands, sniffed the sweet-smelling steam that rose from it, took a sip, closed his eyes, and sighed. "I can't eat until I wake up all the way."

"When's that—like, noon?" I teased as we walked down the road.

With Packrat on one side of me and Roy on the other, I felt pretty lucky. How many kids got to have two of their closest friends living in their backyard all summer? Packrat and I were more like brothers than friends. We got to swim, boat, hike, and just plain hang out together every day.

Roy and I got along a lot better now than when he'd first come here with his mom as a seasonal camper a few summers ago. We'd gotten off to a bad start when his mom found him missing from his tent one night. I knew he had gone fishing for hornpout even though he wasn't allowed to go out alone in a boat at night without permission. My dad made me rat on him.

I looked at Roy out of the corner of my eye. It had taken him forever to forgive me. Sometimes I wondered if he really had, or if maybe we had just come to a truce.

Which might be why I still don't always tell him everything about everything.

Roy and his mom still had a seasonal spot in the campground, like Packrat. But Roy's mom took him kicking and screaming back to Portland every other week for a couple of days. When Packrat and I once asked him why, he'd hinted that his dad didn't like camping, and stayed in the city to work. Roy hadn't talked about his dad since.

When we reached an intersection, Roy headed toward the maintenance area. He and my dad were making picnic tables today. Twenty of them. Roy turned to walk backwards. Pointing at us, he called out, "Catch up with you later. Have fun!"

Fun? *Fun?* He knew we had to clean bathrooms.

"I hope you hit your thumb with a hammer!" I called back.

"I hope you have a full ladies' room!" Roy said.

We heard him chuckle as he turned back around. He knew I'd rather hit my thumb with a hammer.

It figured. The ladies' room was full of ladies. Or maybe there were only two. But the way they talked nonstop, it sounded like it was full. From the utility room between the men's and ladies' rooms, we gave our usual warning knock on the ladies' door.

"Bathroom cleaners!" I yelled.

"Not yet!" a voice yelled back.

Another hollered, "Just a minute!"

We knew "a minute" was really girl-speak for half an hour, so we unlocked the utility door to the men's room. I'd just finished wiping the toilets and checking the toilet paper supply when we heard a shower start on the ladies' side.

"Great!" Packrat said, wiping the last of the three sinks with his washrag.

I dropped the mop in the bucket so hard, water sloshed over the sides. "What takes them so long?"

"I don't want to know."

"Being cooped up in here, not knowing what those guys are doing out there, it's—" I pointed to the bathroom door.

"—driving me crazy, too," Packrat said, grabbing the glass cleaner spray bottle from the supplies. Then he hesitated and asked, "Should I go get Oscar?"

I grinned at the thought of clearing the ladies' room with my three-legged frog. Holding out a hand to take the spray cleaner from him, I said, "Yeah! We haven't used him yet this year."

I sprayed the giant mirror behind the countertop of three sinks, then balled up some paper towels to wipe it down. As I stretched to reach the top, the photos shifted in my back pocket. Knowing those eagle parts were worth so much money was driving me nuts. Why were they so expensive? The pieces were kinda old-looking. Used. Not good enough to put under a piece of glass in a museum or something.

The door to the outside opened. "Did you find him?" I asked.

Looking into the mirror where Packrat's head should have been, I saw a T-shirt-covered chest. A big square chest. I raised my eyes.

"Did I find who?" Mikey asked.

Chapter 11

Bald eagles may appear tough, but they can be harassed off the nest or chased through the air by smaller birds, such as flycatchers, crows, grackles, or even chickadees.

Moose stepped up beside Mikey. He was walking kind of funny. He leaned on one leg, then the other, making a weird face every time he moved.

"Did I find who?" Mikey asked again.

"We're . . . we're closed for cleaning." I squeezed the rolled-up ball of paper towels that was still in my right hand as I tried to keep my voice steady.

Moose groaned as he shifted back onto his other leg.

"We aren't here to use the bathroom," Mikey said, ignoring the weird noises his brother was making. "We're looking for you."

I swear they could hear my knees knocking. "For me?"

Moose put a hand to the small of his back and made a face at me.

"For you." Mikey tilted his own head from one side to the other, and then, using the palm of his hand, pushed up on his chin. I heard a crack, and he sighed in relief.

Where was Packrat? I slid my pointer finger to the trigger of the window cleaner. "Why?"

Moose shuffled his feet again, and gave a low moan. "I don't think I can stand for another minute! Hiking and searching. Searching and hiking. Everything hurts! Isn't there anyplace to sit down?"

I couldn't help it; I snickered.

Mikey looked up at the ceiling, then turned to Moose. "Really? Look around you."

Moose grinned. "Oh yeah!" He limped into the middle stall. Sitting on the closed toilet seat, he held the door open with one hand, then nodded to his brother. "Go ahead."

"If you think you're ready now," Mikey said nicely, though his face looked more like he wanted to flush his brother down the toilet he was sitting on. "You need anything else? Some ice for your feet? A drink?"

Moose put one foot up on his other knee and slid off what looked like a brand-new hiking boot.

Ha! No wonder his feet hurt, I thought. *Serves him right.*

Still holding the door open with one hand, Moose wiggled his toes inside his sock. "I could really use a good foot rub . . ."

"I'm being sarcastic!" Mikey yelled.

"Oh." Moose actually looked sad.

Mikey sighed. To me, he said, "Listen, kid—you built that geocache trail. You walk it all the time. Where would a lost box get to?"

"If I knew, it wouldn't be lost."

He glared at me. "You say you don't have it? Okay. Fine. But it didn't just disappear, kid. And we saw you running away with a box."

"I showed you what was in that—in my box," I said, trying not to cringe at the memory of the first time we'd opened the illegal box. "I bet whoever has your box is long gone by now."

Moose was still rubbing his foot. "We've hiked that trail up and back for two days. We looked in every stone wall. Every hole in a tree big enough to hold a box. Even that old cellar hole. We never found a thing, Mikey. Maybe the kid's right."

Mikey closed his eyes for a second, then looked back over his shoulder at Moose. "I can smell your foot from here, you . . ." Mikey paused. He gave me a questioning look, then whipped back around to look at Moose.

Moose stopped rubbing his foot. "What? What'd I do?"

"What's that? On the floor?"

Moose put both feet on the floor and looked between them.

"No! In the stall next to you." Mikey strode forward to get it.

I saw it now, too. A small, rectangular piece of paper lay on the floor. White edges. Bright yellow, brown, and light tan colors. Without thinking, I dropped the window cleaner and paper towels to check my back pocket. The photos were sticking halfway out—and one must have fallen on the floor! I stuffed them back in and pulled my sweatshirt over them just as Mikey reached the photo and picked it up. He sucked in a breath.

"Where'd this come from?" he barked, storming back toward me.

"I don't know!" I backed up until I was pressed against the counter, wishing I still had the spray bottle in my hand. "Honest! I just got here. We only cleaned the sinks."

Mikey waved the photo in my face. Moose stood behind him, looking over his shoulder. "I wanna see!"

It was my picture of the eagle claw. With my hand next to it, and on my wrist, my blue-and-black survival bracelet. To make things worse, the claw lay on my Wilder Family Campground sweatshirt, and you could see *Wild* and half of Maxwell's head from the pocket logo. I lucked out, not wearing the sweatshirt today! But I *was* wearing the bracelet. Hands behind my back, I pulled my sleeve over it.

Right then, Packrat burst through the door. "Got him! Now we can get rid of those ladies, clean the bathroom, and figure out what to do with—"

He stopped short, staring from me to Mikey to Moose and back.

Mikey looked down at Packrat's cupped hands. "What have you got there?"

"Nothing," Packrat insisted.

Of course, Oscar picked that moment to croak.

I quickly said, "It's just my frog."

"Hey!" Moose moved next to Packrat. "It's only got three legs."

"Cooper saved it, when it got run over."

Mikey nodded. "So it's kind of special," he said.

Before I knew it, Mikey had pocketed the photo, taken Packrat's hands in his own, and pulled them apart. Moose grabbed Oscar and moved away from us.

"Awww . . ." Moose took his pointer finger and rubbed between Oscar's eyes. "He's so cute!"

"Leave him alone! Give him back!" I tried to push past Mikey, but he put an open hand on my chest and held me in place.

"I'll give him back when you promise to help us look for the box. I know it's here somewhere."

"It's not!" *And that's the truth,* I thought. *It's in the canyon.*

"That photo proves it's here. Someone in this campground has it, and you're going to search every square inch until you find it."

Packrat gave me a startled look. "Why us?"

"Because we'd look suspicious walking onto other people's camp-sites and into buildings where we don't belong. You kids are all over the place."

"I'm not helping *you*," I said.

Mikey simply snapped his fingers. Moose stepped into the stall with Oscar. He opened the lid to the toilet and held Oscar over it as the stall door slowly closed.

Whoosh! The sound of flushing water filled the room.

I rushed forward. "No!"

Packrat cried, "You can't do that!"

Mikey got between us and the stall door. As the flushing sound slowly faded, I imagined Oscar swirling around and around and around the toilet bowl, until his little back leg got sucked into the funnel. I stood on my tiptoes, trying to see over or around Mikey, and through the crack in the stall door, but the goon was a brick wall!

Finally, he leaned back and tossed the door open with one hand.

Moose still held Oscar over the toilet by one front foot. I swear that frog shot me a give-them-anything-they-want look.

"What's it gonna be?" Mikey snarled, raising an eyebrow.

What choice did I have? I knew where the box was. I couldn't give it to them; it wasn't theirs. And if I admitted to having it all along, who knows what they'd do.

But, wait. Mikey wanted us to *look* for it. He still didn't know we had it. I could stall for time by pretending.

"Fine," I said.

"Fine, flush the toad? Or fine, you'll search the campground?"

"He's a bullfrog! And we'll search."

The door opened and Gavin strode in. "Hey! I've been looking—" He stopped short, his eyes widening as he took everything in. The door slammed shut behind him.

No one moved. No one said a word for what seemed like five minutes, but was probably thirty seconds.

"Like, what the heck's going on?" Gavin said, slowly pulling his phone from his pocket.

Mikey said, "Oh, my brother was just having some fun with the boys here."

"Putting a bullfrog in a toilet bowl isn't funny! Any cleaners in there will kill it, or make it sick."

Mikey waved a hand at Moose. "That's what I told him. Give the frog back. Don't tease these nice boys anymore."

"But Mikey!" Moose pouted, as he handed me back my frog.

"No buts! Now let's go."

As the door slammed shut behind them, Gavin said, "What's up with them?"

I checked Oscar out and gave a sigh of relief to see he wasn't hurt at all.

"They didn't like finding a frog in the bathroom," I lied.

Chapter 12

Eagles cannot see well at night.

"Whoa, whoa, whoa." One of our regular camp kids pointed at Packrat, who leaned against the little kids' climber with his hands in the pockets of his coat, a big smile on his face. "Why do *you* three always get to be on the same team? It's not fair."

It was the same argument we had every Manhunt game since Packrat, Roy, and I had started teaming up. One dim playground light shone down on the group of kids, who stood in a circle waiting for the teams to be called so they could race off into the dark beyond to hide and seek. Several of them grumbled in agreement with the kid.

"Okay," I said to the kid. "I'll go on your team." It still wouldn't be fair teams, because Packrat and Roy were good at Manhunt. Very, very good. But it would keep the kids happy. Customer service and all that.

The drizzly rain from this morning had stopped. The air was still damp enough to wet my hair down and seep into my sneakers, but it was warmer, too. I smiled to hear the peepers calling loudly from the lake beyond the tree line, even as I slapped at a mosquito buzzing in my ear.

"Hey!" Roy brought my mind back to the playground. "I'll take Matt."

I smiled. "I've got Ty."

Roy and I divided up the rest of the kids who wanted in on the game. Then he ran through the rules, just 'cause we knew from experience that not everyone plays Manhunt the same way. When you've got kids coming and going all summer long from all over the state, and even the country, the best way to make sure no one was calling anyone else a cheater was to lay all the rules out for them right off the bat.

Cooper and Packrat: Mystery of the Eagle's Nest

"That climber," Roy said, pointing into the shadows, "is home. If you're tagged before you get to it, you're sent to jail under the basketball hoop until you're tagged by someone from your team."

"Anything out of bounds?" a kid asked.

"You have to stay inside the inner loop of roads. No hiding at the lake. No jumping the fence to the pool." Roy turned to point at me. "No hiding in the bathrooms." A couple of kids chuckled, remembering the last time I'd been on a team separate from Roy and Packrat. I'd hidden in the ladies' room, holding a mop and bucket. I'd told all the women someone had gotten sick and the bathroom was closed until I got it cleaned up. Roy and Packrat had looked for me for an hour until they overheard a lady complain about how long it was taking "that young man" to clean up in there.

Packrat moved to stand in front of me. We each held a fist in the air, pumping it on every word we chanted, "Rock, paper, scissors—go!"

I held out a sideways peace sign. Packrat flashed an open hand.

"We hide first!" I called.

"One, two, three . . ." Packrat began to count.

Everyone scattered, except me. I'd had a plan since this morning.

". . . eight, nine, ten . . ." Packrat's voice was muffled now, his head in his sleeve up against a maple-tree trunk.

I jogged toward the back of the store. In just a few steps, I was plunged into total darkness. It took a minute for my eyes to adjust, but I knew this campground like a fox knows its territory, so I didn't have to slow down much.

The back of the store had no windows at all. A shortcut path ran between it and a twelve-foot-tall row of hedges. This made it one of the darkest spots in the campground. I leaned up against the store and glanced down the path. Not hearing or seeing anyone, I slid my way along the building. Halfway down, I bumped into something hard.

When it jumped away from me, I almost yelled, but a familiar voice said, "Cooper?"

Pounding footsteps and voices from the kids on my team who were still trying to find a hiding spot had me grabbing his shirt and pulling him down into a crouch.

"*Shhhhhh!*" I warned, recognizing Gavin now. "Don't give me away!" My plan wouldn't work with a ton of kids. And besides, I knew that right now, Roy was standing on top of the kids' climber, trying to see who was hiding in which direction.

"Are you in trouble?" he whispered back. "Are those guys after you?"

I dropped to all fours before answering. "Yes! They want to put me in jail."

"In jail?" he said.

"*Shhhhhh!*" I said, more loudly than I planned. The voices stopped. Then someone asked someone else if they'd seen where I'd gone. The someone else said they hadn't.

Gavin chuckled. "Manhunt."

I rolled my eyes—not that he could see it or anything.

"I haven't played in forever . . ." he began.

I ignored him and crawled forward to quietly push through a break in the hedge, hoping he'd get the hint. Instead, he pulled on the bottom of my jeans. "There's gotta be better places to hide than this," he suggested from behind me. "Your parents have a campfire. It's all lit up."

Like I didn't know how to play Manhunt!

"I'm not hiding at the campfire," I hissed. I tugged hard to get him to let go and nodded to the left of us. "I'm hiding in that."

Up against this side of the hedge was the woodshed. It stood about four feet high and twelve feet long. The front doors, normally locked against wood thieves, stood wide open. I couldn't see one stick of wood in that shed, but I knew it was there. I'd stacked it myself this morning, fort-like, with Manhunt in mind.

Straight in front of us, about forty feet away, the fire burned bright. But its light only reached to the circle of chairs around it and the people who sat in them, chatting back and forth. If I could get in the shed without the adults calling out to me, I knew I'd have the best hiding spot ever.

Better than the ladies' room, even.

I moved forward. The sound of jeans dragging through the dirt and leaves came from behind me. I sighed. Gavin.

"I lead," I told him. "Stick close to the hedge and move real slow," I whisper-warned. "And *no* talking!"

Gavin's teeth glowed when he grinned back at me.

I glanced once at the campfire. No one was paying us any attention. Good. I moved my hands in front of me to clear any sticks or twigs out of the way before we knelt on them.

"Here we come!" Packrat's voice carried beyond the playground exactly as he wanted it to. Voices rang out, this time by the seekers as they spread out to search for us like a coyote hunts its prey at night.

Chapter 13

Bald eagles lay two, or sometimes three, eggs. The eaglets hatch five weeks later, and begin to fly ten to twelve weeks after that.

Gavin and I were only ten feet from the best hiding spot ever when Dad stood up from his chair. We moved back into the hedge as far as we could, trying to blend into the shadows. His back to us, Dad wrapped a hand around his black poker, which always hung on a nearby tree, and used it to move the logs in the fire. Orange sparks shot up from the fire ring, then floated in the air.

Was he going for more wood, or wasn't he?

"A perfect night for a fire," he announced to the group.

Everyone nodded, and the campfire weather chat began. I eyed Dad carefully, trying to figure out if he was stretching or getting the fire ready for more wood. When he kept poking at the fire and talking, I inched toward the shed a little more.

Pounding sneakers! Roy's and Packrat's Manhunt team were coming our way! I dropped flat to the ground, then slid half under the hedge. My shirt bunched up under my rib cage, and last year's dried-up leaves, pine needles, and twigs scratched and poked my stomach. I shifted a tiny bit, trying to get rid of them, but that only made it worse.

Don't move, don't breathe. Don't move, don't breathe.

The running steps came closer. Closer still. Then they stopped right on the other side of the hedge.

Soft, light, tickling movements started on my wrist. A beetle. An ant?

The footsteps moved to the left a few steps. The tickling feeling was at my elbow. A spider? I shuddered.

The steps came back even with us. The tickling was halfway to my shoulder. Another second and it'd be inside my shirt, in my armpit!

"No one over here!" yelled the voice that went with the footsteps, and they took off again.

Gavin snorted softly as we rolled out from under the hedge. I swatted at my arm, smiling at our close call.

The loons wailed, keeping in touch with each other and their two babies. Everyone at the campfire stopped talking to look toward the lake. It didn't matter that you couldn't see it from here; the call of the loon pulled you toward it, made you wish you were out there with them.

"Has anyone been out on the lake lately?" Mom asked.

Lucy's voice spoke up. "I knew there was something I wanted to tell you! I was out there today, and I watched the eagle harassing a loon!"

"They do that from time to time," Dad said.

"Can an eagle pick up a loon?" Packrat's mom asked.

Gavin snorted. I didn't get why that was a funny question; I'd been asked it lots of times.

Dad answered, "Well, the adult loons dive and stay under for a pretty long time. Eagles couldn't get their talons on one easily, that's for sure. And if they did, they probably couldn't lift it. But they could steal a *baby* loon in the blink of an eye."

Several people gasped in amazement. Dad kept poking the fire.

"A wildlife biologist visited during our first year running the place, to band the eagle chicks. Took Cooper with him, too. The guy climbed the tree and lowered the babies down in a burlap bag for the team on the ground to band them. While he was up there, he took some samples from the nest, like feathers, fur, and bones. They did find the bones of a full-size turkey; not sure how they got that up there."

"Probably in pieces," said a deep, slow-talking voice. After the chatter about turkey pieces died down, the deep voice added, "I've been out to see their nest. It's quite remarkable."

I moved toward the campfire very quietly, squinting through the shadows. Who was that? Was that Gavin's dad? Dad poked the fire again and the man's face lit up. No—it was Hawke. The Native American guy from the store with the GPS and the directions and—

"Is it an old nest?" Hawke asked.

Mom spoke this time. "Our neighbors," she paused, a sad look crossing her face. "The couple that *were* our neighbors, they told us the eagles stole it from the osprey nine years ago."

Another voice cut in. "There are eagles on this lake?"

I gasped, noticing two things at the same time. One: The goons had joined the campfire; and two: I swore Hawke glanced in my direction when they did.

I quietly slid back into the hedge.

Pounding footsteps were coming our way. I felt the tugs Gavin gave to my shirt, but those goons were at my parents' campfire, acting all chummy-chummy. With everybody!

Mom's hands cupped her favorite mug, the one with the loon etched on it. She leaned forward to put her elbows on her knees. "After all the hiking you did today, you never saw them?"

Mikey shook his head. "Nah. We were too busy looking for all those geocaches."

"Your kid's pretty good at hiding them." Moose sounded a little like Molly when she'd been stuck in the store with Mom too long.

"They did have clever hiding spots," Mr. Valley said.

From the other side of the hedge came giggles and calls. Four or five kids, maybe Packrat leading them, running together, hunting us down.

"Cooper's the last one!" a kid called.

Reluctantly, I let Gavin pull me toward the woodshed, but I kept one ear toward the fire.

"It's not often you see four eagle chicks in one nest," Hawke commented.

Dad stopped stirring the campfire. Mom's cup paused halfway to her lips. I stepped on a twig, sending a faint crack through the air. No one at the campfire heard it though, 'cause they were all talking one over the other.

"Four?"

"You're mistaken. It's three. You saw three."

"That's impossible."

Hawke's chuckles were a deep rumble. "No, I'm sure. Here. I have a picture on my camera."

I whispered to myself, "Not possible."

Behind me, Gavin whispered, "Rare, but possible. There have only been four sets of quadruplets in the United States since biologists started keeping records."

I clenched my fists and ignored the know-it-all, even though part of me wanted to pound him with questions.

Several people jumped up to look over Hawke's shoulder, including my parents. I so badly wanted to join them, but I didn't dare. Instead, I backed up to be swallowed by the darkness of the shed.

"It could be——" Mom said.

"I don't know; it looks like a stick to me," Lucy argued.

"But it's not in this photo," Moose pointed out.

Hawke patiently passed his camera around. "If it were the last egg laid, there would be several days between seeing the first couple of eaglets and this one. It takes a few weeks for their legs to be steady enough to carry them, too. That's why you haven't noticed it until now."

"Imagine that," Mom breathed. "Quadruplets!"

Quadruplets. *Quadruplets!* It was so cool. I had to get out on the lake tomorrow to see them! I'd never heard of such a thing. Three was rare, but four?

"Oh, but what's the littlest one's chance of survival?" Gavin's dad asked. "My son tells me the older eaglets will sometimes pick on the younger ones. And if the oldest is a week older, he'll be stronger . . ."

His words hung in the air like the gray smoke from the fire.

Hawke said softly, "Hatchlings have about a fifty percent chance of surviving their first year. With four crowded in the nest, that percentage would drop. Doesn't seem like the littlest one would have much of a chance at all, does it?"

"Why?" asked Packrat's mom, whose eyes were shiny with tears.

"Lots of reasons," Hawke said, putting out his hand palm up, as if he was offering them to the crowd. "Because there's not enough room in the nest. Chicks grow quickly, and at two months, they're almost adult-size." He thought for a moment. "One could get pushed out of the nest by another. It could spread its wings and be taken by a gust of wind. If it's not fed fast enough or if food is scarce, the weakest will be attacked by its own siblings for a bigger share. Then there's the nest's location. Too much sun, and they could get dehydrated."

Moose grinned. "Hmm . . . Maybe we should take one of the chicks off the parents' hands. Sounds like we'd be saving the poor little thing."

I gasped, then clamped a hand over my own mouth. People around the campfire cleared their throats and shuffled in their seats, so I didn't think anyone had heard me. Gavin stared unblinkingly at the group.

In the flickering campfire light, I saw Dad give Mom one of his did-I-just-hear-what-I-thought-I-heard? looks. Mom shot back an I-can't-imagine-why-he'd-say-that look.

Lucy laughed. "You can't be serious. I'm sure stealing an eagle baby is some kind of federal offense."

Mikey stared hard at Moose. "Of course it's an offense. He was just kidding, weren't you, Moose?"

Moose's grin drooped. "A bad joke. Sorry."

Dad and Mom and Lucy exchanged I-told-you-so looks.

Through the whole conversation, Hawke had been studying Mikey and Moose like an owl studies its surroundings.

"Interesting idea, though, gentlemen. Interesting."

Chapter 14

The average life span of an eagle is twenty-eight years in the wild—and thirty-six years in captivity.

The campfire talk about taking an eaglet off the eagle parents' hands still rang in my ears. On the other side of the hedge, Packrat and Roy ran past Gavin and me. A kid yelled to them that we were hiding behind the game room and they needed seekers to surround us. I came really close, even reached out a hand to pull them into the hedge to tell them what we'd heard. But I realized they'd tag Gavin and me out first, only listening to what we had to say second.

Plus, they'd never let me live down a Manhunt loss. It could wait ten minutes.

I glanced toward my perfect hiding spot, the one I'd so carefully built this morning. I'd piled the wood in a wall toward the front of the shed, leaving room to squeeze in over the top and hide behind it. They never would have found me there; they would have searched for me forever.

Only I didn't have forever right now. I needed to end this game.

Gavin and I got all the way down on the ground to crawl carefully forward across the dirt and leaves. Past the back side of the woodshed. Through a small grouping of trees.

Reaching a couple of good-size bushes, with a two-foot-long log lying on the ground in amongst them, Gavin and I crouched to stake out the playground. Lifting our heads to peek at the guards and the climber, I chuckled softly. "This will be way too easy!"

Between us and home base were two kids from the other team. Standing half in and half out of the shadows, one of them kept throwing his flashlight in the air and catching it. And it was switched on! The other played with his iPod, headphones in his ears. Talk about standing out like brown rabbits on white snow!

I shifted from kneeling on my right knee to kneeling on my left. *Oww!* A sharp pain ran through it. I grabbed it with my hand and groaned, seeing the sharp stick I'd knelt on. Gavin ducked, and I realized the kid with the flashlight had heard me. He swung the beam in our direction. I dropped to the ground.

The beam from the kid's light came closer and closer and closer, just grazing the log before he pulled it back.

"Whew!" I whispered to Gavin. He grinned my way. We slid along the ground until we'd gotten behind the next group of bushes and maple saplings. Suddenly, the kids' voices got a little louder. Then a little louder still. We slowly raised our heads until we saw them through the tree branches.

Gavin gave me a look and I shrugged my shoulders. "No clue," I whispered.

Flashlight kid stood tall. "Fine; we do it again. I go first." He lifted his chin a little, took a deep breath, and started burping. *Buuuuuuuurp!*

"Is that all you got?" said the other kid. He took a swallow of something from a red can—Coke, maybe. "Listen to this!" *BuuuuuuuUURRRRP!*

I snorted loudly, then buried my mouth and nose in my hands. Roy and Packrat let these two clowns guard home base? My stomach hurt from holding in the laughs. Tears balled up in my eyes. Peeking again, I could see how serious this kid was about his burping technique. Almost as serious as his friend, who'd now reached for his own soda can.

My body shook from the inside out. I looked over at Gavin. He was curled up in a ball, arms wrapped around his stomach like he'd just eaten a bad piece of fish. "Amateurs!" He half-snorted the word, half-whispered it.

"Hey! Who's out there?" The flashlight beam was waving all over the place over our heads, and coming closer and closer.

This was it. We were gonna have to run for it now. No time to plan.

"Get ready," I said.

Gavin whispered, "Wait. I've got an idea."

He went into a crouch, brushing his knees off as he stared at the kids.

I whispered, "Are you crazy? You'll give us away!"

He grinned. "I'm giving *me* away. But I'm not on any team. It doesn't really matter if I get home or not, right? Wait here. You'll know when it's time to go."

Crouching as low as he could, he moved forward about ten feet, then silently stood up, and made a run for the climber.

But he didn't really look like he was trying to make it there.

Flashlight kid saw him first. "Hey! He's going for home! Get him!"

The friend reached him first, easily tagging him on the back. Gavin put his hands in the air and turned around. "You got me! I couldn't find the climber."

The boys took a closer look. Flashlight kid shone the light in Gavin's face, which had Gavin leaning back and squinting at him. "I don't remember you."

The two kids each took an arm and led him to the back of the playground to jail, which was under the basketball hoop—and farther away from the climber. I smiled to myself.

Gavin said more loudly than he needed to, "Hey, I heard some awesome burps coming from this direction. Which one of you was it?"

"That was me!" Flashlight kid then got shoved by this friend, who declared he was full of it; Gavin was talking about *his* burp.

"I can do you one better," Gavin boasted. He leaned in close to the kids. I couldn't quite hear what he was saying, but then flashlight kid burst out laughing. "No way!" he said.

"Yes, way," Gavin put a hand in the air. "Honest. I even did it in a talent show. Took first place."

"Show us!" said the other kid.

Gavin stood tall, squared his shoulders, and gave an enormous burp that probably had the people at the campfire turning to look. Not just any burp either. He was burping the alphabet!

"*Ccccc . . . Dddddd . . . EeeeeEEEEe . . .*"

The kids cheered him on, not paying any attention to the goal, the flashlight pointed at the ground.

I moved slowly from tree to tree, standing taller as I went. The climber was close. I had this!

"*HhhhhhH, IIIIIiiiiii, Jj, KKKKKkkk . . .*"

I glanced over toward the jail. Gavin's face was all screwed up, eyes huge, one hand on his stomach, concentrating on burping the letter *L*.

I sighed. I had to get Gavin home, too.

"Just a couple letters more," I whispered, feeling along the ground for anything heavy. *There!* A rock; two of them. I lifted them and threw the first over Gavin's head into the bushes behind him.

"Wait!" Flashlight kid looked past Gavin into the woods. I threw the second rock, and he and his friend stormed into the trees, shining the flashlight every which way.

Gavin kept going, really exaggerating the noises now: "*LIIIIIIIILLLL, Mmmmmmm, Nnnnn, OOOOOOOOOO—*"

The flashlight beam was still in the woods behind Gavin.

I took off. Gavin saw me coming and went to the very edge of the imaginary jail wall to stretch out his hand. I slapped it and turned on one foot to run for the climber. Gavin's footsteps in the sand marked time with mine. "Coooooooper! Run, kid, run!"

Flashlight kid and his friend were coming after us now. I heard one of them say, "Cooper? He's the sneaky one Roy said to watch out for!"

Their flashlight beam hit me, but it was too late. I grinned to myself as I quickly closed the distance between home and me. I was going to make it! I lunged toward the climber. Four feet to go. Three feet. Two.

Roy! Barreling toward me on the right. Could I make it? His grin proved he didn't think so.

My fingers inches from the climber, and Roy's, inches from my shoulder, he yelled, "Got—"

Suddenly, I felt a shove on my left shoulder. I flew forward to slap home. Seconds later, Gavin's hand landed next to mine, while Roy stumbled past our backs in a blur to land in the sand.

"Yes!" I shouted, jumping up and punching the air with my fist.

Gavin and I high-fived. He clapped me on the back.

"We make a good team!" he said.

"You had a great plan!" I had to admit.

"But you added to it!" He sighed happily. "I can't remember the last time I had so much fun on a playground."

Roy stood up from where he'd fallen and brushed off his pants.

Packrat jogged into the light. "You got lucky!" he said to me, but he shot me a grin too.

"I would have had you if Gavin hadn't cheated and saved your butt," Roy grumbled. "He isn't even playing!"

Gavin grinned at Roy and Packrat. "I made sure I had Cooper's back."

My radio crackled. "Shoot!" Turning the volume up, I pushed the button. "What?"

"Cooper!" Mom's voice. I should have known. "Where are you? You were supposed to check in an hour ago."

I smiled. If she only knew how close I'd been to her for the last hour. "Sorry! We were playing Manhunt, and I lost track of time."

Roy's snort turned my grin into a frown. He never got into any trouble for not checking in. Ever! Me, I got hour-long ground-ations if I was fifteen minutes late. But all Roy had to do was give a good reason. Half the time, he was home before his mom even realized he was late. Why couldn't my mom be more like Roy's mom?

"Who are you with?" she asked.

I sighed a long sigh.

"Don't sigh at me," she said. I rolled my eyes. "And no eye rolls either!"

The guys laughed out loud this time. How did she do that? And *why* did she do that?

"I'm with Packrat and Roy. And Gavin."

Her tone instantly softened. "Gavin? Good! I knew you'd like him. Do you need another hour?"

I hesitated. Was this a trick question? "Umm . . ."

"He's a good kid, and he's older. He'll look after you."

She made him sound like a babysitter. Gavin ducked his head to study his shoe, drawing a square in the sand.

I turned my back on the guys and stormed away about ten steps. Putting my hand over my mouth and the radio, I whispered, "*Mom!* You're embarrassing me! I don't need looking after!"

"Sorry. But I worry. It's what we moms do. And Gavin is—" I heard a sleepy-little-girl voice before my radio went silent. Then Mom was back. "Sorry, Coop. I can hear through her monitor that Molly just woke up. I've got to run inside and check on her. Have fun with your friends."

Have fun with my friends. What was I, six?

When I got back to the group, all the Manhunt kids had broken up to go to the game room or to take a walk around the campground or to get an ice cream or something. Packrat and Roy were sitting on the swings, rocking side to side. Every now and then, their swings would bump into each other. I wanted to tell them about the eagles and what I'd heard, but Gavin was standing right there, and I didn't want him butting in on the plans I'd been hatching.

"So what do you think about those guys talking about taking an eaglet?" Gavin asked me.

So much for keeping him out of it.

"What?" Roy stopped swinging.

At the same time Packrat asked, "Guys?"

I downplayed it as I told them what Mikey, Moose, and Hawke had said at the campfire. "Nobody took them seriously, though," I added at the end, hoping they'd drop it until Gavin left.

"What would they want with an eaglet?" Packrat asked. "We didn't read anything about eaglet—"

I tapped his foot with mine to remind him that Gavin didn't know about any of that.

"What if they stole one, nursed it to adulthood, and then killed it for its parts?" Roy suggested.

I groaned quietly. But Gavin didn't even bat an eye at that. He simply said, "There might be other . . . well . . . *uses* for a baby eagle."

Curiosity got the better of me. "Like what?" I asked.

"Well, like, I read somewhere that some cultures think eating an eaglet will give them healing properties."

"Ewww!" Packrat said. "Not in Maine!"

Gavin shrugged, then pulled out his phone. Glancing at it, he then used it like a flashlight. "I've got to get back to the camper. See you tomorrow?"

"Sure," Roy said.

"I think I've got to work," I said. "But maybe."

I didn't hear what Packrat said. I was too busy thinking about the eagle family and watching Gavin walk away.

"Those eaglets are fifty feet in the air," Roy scoffed as he twirled his swing until the chains twisted, then lifted his feet so he would spin. "They can't touch them."

I put my hands in my pockets and hung my head. Quietly, I said, "Yes, they can."

Roy jumped off his swing and turned to face me. "It sounded like you said they can."

"Two years ago, they came to band the eaglets," I explained, with the same story my dad had just told the campers. "The biologist climbed the tree with nothing but a rope and spiked shoes. He put an eaglet into a burlap bag and lowered it to the ground. The other biologist took it out of the bag, clamped a red tag on one leg and a silver tag on the other, took blood to test for mercury, took some measurements, then put it back in the bag. The biologist at the top of the tree lifted it up and put it back in the nest." I took a deep breath.

"It's possible," I said. "Very possible."

Chapter 15

During the first nine days of its life, an eaglet cannot focus its eyes.

The next morning, I searched the bathrooms, the maintenance area, the workshop, and even the pool (although that was a long shot) for Dad before Mom finally told me he was fixing a water leak on site 10. Hawke's site.

"Maybe I can help you?" she asked.

I slowly backed toward the door. "Nooo . . ."

"Are you sure?" She wore her best you-can-tell-me smile.

"It's more of a guy question." My hands pushed on the screen door and I was gone in a flash. She would have thrown too many questions my way after she'd heard the one I wanted to ask. Dad, though—he always asked just enough.

I stepped onto the site, then followed Dad's whistling to the back, where I found his feet sticking out from under the motor home.

"Hey, Dad. How's it going?" I squatted lower to the ground.

"Cooper? Glad you showed up! Hand me a Phillips-head screw-driver, please. I need to tighten this clamp." His hand came out from under the motor home, palm up.

I poked around the red metal toolbox, which sat open right in front of me.

"What's up?" he asked. "You and Packrat and Roy, you seem pretty busy lately."

"Yeah." Finding the screwdriver, I put it into Dad's hand. "A cache went missing, and we're trying to replace it."

"Oh," he said, distractedly. "Hey, it's really something about those eaglets, huh? You must be pretty excited. Your mom looked it up and there's only been, like, four cases of quadruplets in the country, ever."

Exactly what Gavin had said. Figured.

I pulled a blade of grass out of the ground and rolled it around in my fingers. "We're going out to try to see them today."

"Good! Take pictures. You know how your mom likes to show them off in the office."

We both fell into silence. I wrestled with myself in my mind. *Do I ask? Don't I?*

Maybe if I half-ask . . .

"What if someone stole something, and you found it. But they don't know you have it."

"You give it back."

"To the thief?"

"No, to the rightful owner." Dad grunted as he turned the screw the last couple of tightening turns. He looked at it, then tightened it one last time. "Are you sure what you found was stolen from another kid?"

"Kid?" The word was out of my mouth before I could stop it.

Dad chuckled. "Just tell me this: Is it expensive—something that's valuable? Like an iPod or a tablet? We're not talking a plastic ring, right?"

I pulled another blade of grass. "Yeah, it's kind of expensive."

Dad's hand appeared again, holding the screwdriver. I reached for it as he spoke, putting it back in the toolbox. "Then you have to give it back. Even if it means one of your friends might get mad at you." Dad slid out from under the motor home and looked up at me while wiping his hands on a rag. He asked, "What if it was something of yours they'd taken?"

I looked at Dad. Should I tell him they were about to take something of ours? Okay, so the eaglets weren't *ours,* but I felt responsible for them. If I had just given back the parts, those goons and their boss wouldn't be targeting the eaglets.

Dad's eyes grew questioning. He stopped wiping his hands. "Coop—"

"Hey there, Jim!" It was Mikey. He smiled at me, eyebrows raised. "Cooper. You two look pretty serious. You're not in trouble, are you, young man? Lose another geocache?"

I balled up my hands. Very slowly, so the dummy would understand, I said, "*I* didn't lose it."

Mikey turned so his back was to Dad. His voice still playful, but with a steely look in his eyes, he said, "Have you found it, though? You've been searching?"

"I've searched," I fibbed carefully. "It's gone."

Dad stood up and put a hand on my shoulder. "I'm sorry to hear that. But don't let it keep you from trying again, okay?"

Mikey put a big smile back on his face. "I hope it turns up. For your sake." To Dad, he said, "I actually came for Hawke. He left a message that he wanted to see me."

Dad shook his head. "He's not here. Coop, can you hand me the wrench?" I did. "Thanks. Now go inside and when I tell you, turn the water on, okay? I need to check for more leaks."

I walked around to the side of the motor home. I heard Dad push himself back under it, and to Mikey, he said, "Hawke's gone into town to run a couple of errands. Should be back in about an hour."

Grabbing the door handle, I pulled it toward me and climbed the three steps inside. It was neat and clean. Not fancy, but new. All browns and tans and gold-colored trim. On the left wall were the kitchen cabinets and stove. On the opposite wall was a soft bench behind a long kitchen table. A couch and recliner faced a thirty-inch TV hanging on the opposite wall.

"Coop?" yelled Dad. "Turn it on."

"Okay!" I turned the kitchen sink faucet handle. Through the window, I heard Mikey ask Dad, "If you're still here when he gets back, could you tell him I stopped by to discuss business?"

I mumbled to myself, "Business? What the heck?"

"Sure, I'll try to remember," Dad said. He yelled to me, "Cooper? Shut it off. Now turn the bathroom sink on, wouldya?"

I walked to the very back of the motor home and opened the door to the bathroom. On the other side of it was another door, half open, leading into the bedroom. I turned left toward the sink, and a flash of red, white, and yellow in the bedroom caught my eye. One hand over the faucet, I froze.

I couldn't help it; I had to see. I put my hand flat on the door and slowly pushed it open. Lying right there on the bed was a very, very old tomahawk. The handle was wrapped in leather, and two beaded, leather strands hung from it. Each of those had an eagle feather tied to it. It was amazing! Beyond amazing! It was the coolest thing I'd ever seen. And it was real. I didn't need an expert to tell me that.

Old, too. Almost like . . . an antique.

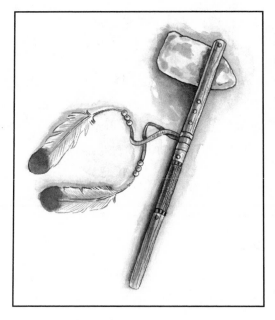

Slowly, I stuck out my hand to touch it. Just when one finger touched the worn, soft, brown leather, I heard from outside, "Coooooooper!"

I jumped a mile and pulled my hand back.

"Did you turn that bathroom water on?"

I'd forgotten about Dad. "Just found it!"

I'd found it all right. Another clue.

Chapter 16

Eagles curl their talons when on the nest, walking on their knuckles, to keep them from accidentally piercing an egg or eaglet.

"Whoa!" Packrat's eyes got bigger and bigger as I described the tomahawk to him. He'd turned around on his canoe bench to look back at me. "Did you get a picture?"

I threw the anchor overboard, then shook my head. "I didn't have my phone with me. I was gonna call you, but after I turned the water on and off, Dad said everything looked good and we were done. I had to leave."

Packrat reached for his fishing pole. "So we have a suspect."

I glanced quickly at Packrat. Then I softly said, "We have two."

"Two?"

"Gavin."

Packrat said, "Wait—I thought you liked him.

"I do like him . . . most of the time," I said quickly, "when he isn't treating us like little kids. But there's still something weird about him."

"He can't be the boss. Millions of dollars are at stake."

"Sure," I said quickly, "but what if his *dad* is the boss? Or the buyer? He's an antiques dealer. I looked in our reservations computer, and they checked in the day before the goons did. Mr. Valley and Gavin walked the trail the day before us. His dad asked a lot of questions at the campfire, too." When Packrat didn't say anything, I added, "What if his dad sent him out to see what we know?"

Packrat tipped his head from side to side like he was thinking *Maybe he's right, maybe he's not.* I said, "Until we know for sure, let's keep the tomahawk between us, okay?"

"And Roy?"

"Uh-uh. He likes Gavin too much. I'm not sure what he's told him already."

Packrat sighed. "Okay. Hey, did you bring any worms?"

I held up Molly's pink pail, which was full of the worms I'd dug first thing this morning.

"Your mom has a cooler full of night crawlers," he said. "Why not just take those?"

"Take them?" I said. "Now that I get a paycheck, she makes me buy them! These are free."

Packrat dug around in the dark, wet dirt with his fingers. He pulled out a worm and tossed it to the side of the pail. "Too small." Then he dug around again and again, until he found one just the right size. Holding the hook in one hand, he slid the worm onto it with the other, all the while screwing up his face with a this-is-going-to-hurt-me-more-than-it-is-you look.

While I hooked my own, he released some line to attach a red-and-white bobber. Fishing rod in his right hand, he leaned it back, then snapped it forward while hitting the release button to let out line. The bobber sailed through the air and plopped in the water thirty yards from the boat.

"Nice cast," I said as I flung my own bobber and worm out.

I sat with one foot on the side of the canoe, watching my bobber go up and down, up and down. The lake was calm, reflecting the shoreline so perfectly that if you squinted and turned your head sideways, you almost couldn't tell which was the reflection and which was dry land.

The sun had begun to make its way down toward the treetops. A loon wailed on one end of the lake. Another answered from behind us.

We weren't really here to fish; we were doing an undercover thing. Checking out the eagle family. We'd been out here for thirty minutes and had only seen two eaglet heads pop up at the same time.

"Do you think they've already gotten one?" I kept looking up at the nest, hoping to see all four eaglets.

"No way," Packrat said, but he didn't really meet my eyes.

The canoe gently bobbed left to right whenever we cast. More and more chirping came from the eagles' nest. Still, we could only see two heads at a time.

An adult eagle sat on the edge of the nest, her back to us and her eaglets. I knew it was the mom, because side by side with the other one, she was a little larger. And the one brown feather on the back of her otherwise pure white head gave her away. Every now and then, when the eaglets were really loud, she'd look up at the sky as if thinking, *He's always late with dinner!*

My bobber went under. I felt a hard tug on my line.

"I think I've got one!" I yelled.

I reeled, then released a little bit of line. Reeled. Released. Reeled, and then I felt the give that told me it had gotten away. "Darn it," I said, reeling the worm in all the way. Well, half the worm. I sighed, hooked another worm, and recast.

A warm breeze blew, the kind that hinted at a hot spell to come. I turned my face into it and closed my eyes. I'd just drifted off to sleep when the eaglets started going nuts above us. My eyes shot open and I twisted in my seat toward the chirping.

"Three heads!" Packrat pointed up at the nest.

Mom eagle turned her head only, looking up and off to her right to a little brown speck soaring toward them. All three eaglets got quiet as they, too, looked up hopefully. The brown speck grew larger and larger still, until we could see its white head and yellow talons.

Its yellow, empty talons.

"Uh-oh," I said, with a grin.

Dad soared the last few yards, talons downward.

Cooper and Packrat: Mystery of the Eagle's Nest

Mom eagle turned away as he landed on the other side of the nest. The eaglets leaned in toward him, though, clamoring for dinner. When Dad folded his wings onto his sides, Mom looked back at him with a fierce how-dare-you-come-home-empty-taloned look, before she took to the sky in search of dinner for her eaglets. Packrat and I chuckled.

Then I saw it.

"Four!" I cried. "There *are* four!"

"Sweet!" Packrat said. "He's a lot smaller than the others," he murmured, squinting up toward the nest. "I hope he makes it."

The biggest one pulled himself across the nest with his beak until he was in front of his father. He kept crying and crying. The adult just looked off into the sky, probably hoping his partner would have better luck.

We were so busy watching those eaglets, we didn't see or hear Roy's rowboat until he and Gavin were almost alongside us.

"They're all there?" Roy asked, after he cut the small outboard motor.

I nodded.

"I'm guessing they're, like, seven weeks old," Gavin said. "Otherwise, both parents would leave them alone to go out and hunt."

Did he expect us to be super-impressed that he knew that?

"Really?" Roy exclaimed. "Very cool!"

Obviously, Roy was.

"Any luck?" Gavin asked, nodding toward our poles.

Packrat and I shook our heads.

"I know a great spot," Roy said. "Follow me."

"Can we still watch the nest?" I asked.

"Sure! It's at the shady end of Ant Island." Roy shaded his eyes and glanced over at the long skinny island that was home to only wildlife. "The left end."

Cooper and Packrat: Mystery of the Eagle's Nest

Once we'd settled into our new fishing spot and everyone had cast their lines, Gavin started to talk about what the goons had said last night. There was no way around it; it would have been wicked rude not to talk at all, so we did. But Roy and Packrat and I did not mention the photos of the eagle parts to Gavin. Packrat and I didn't mention the tomahawk to Roy and Gavin. No one talked about the box in the canyon. Things were getting a little complicated.

But there was one thing we all agreed on: The eaglets had to be watched.

"How are you going to do it?" Gavin asked me. "You three can't be here fishing every minute of every day—and what about nighttime?"

I looked back toward the eagles' nest, then at the Wentworths' lawn. Slowly paddling past it was a familiar-looking canoe. I shaded my eyes with my hands, but I still couldn't tell who it was.

"*Shhhhhh!*" I told Roy and Gavin, who were still talking about protecting the eaglets. "Packrat?"

"Already on it," he said. Hands elbow deep in a coat pocket, he pulled out a pair of binoculars and handed them to me, then raised a second pair to his own eyes.

"It's one of ours," I said, meaning a campground rental canoe.

Gavin leaned forward to try to get a better look. "Who's in it?"

"Hawke."

"I don't need binoculars to know who those big guys are with him," Roy spat out.

We quietly paddled closer to the island, farther into its shade. We weren't invisible, but I wanted to watch them before they saw us.

Hawke pointed up at the nest. Mikey and Moose shaded their eyes, gazing up at it. The three men seemed comfortable with each other. Hawke stayed quiet and serious while Mikey and Moose laughed every now and again.

I nibbled on my lip. They were staking out the nest!

"I think," I said quietly, "we're going to have to camp out under it."

"Cool!" Roy's eyes lit up at my idea. "Think your mom will go for it, though?"

Mom. Leave it to Roy to remember how my mom babied me.

"I'm not sure my mom will go for it either," Packrat said quickly.

"Unless," Roy grinned at us, "you two told your moms Gavin was with us!"

"But . . . what?" Gavin practically shouted the two words.

Hawke and Mikey and Moose looked our way.

Gavin looked from me, to their canoe, then back to the three of us. "Umm, I don't know—"

Hawke raised a hand in greeting. Gavin raised his quickly, and only halfway. Mikey and Moose stared between the two of them. So did Roy, Packrat, and I.

Gavin and Hawke knew each other well enough to wave?

"I can't go with you," Gavin said, looking everywhere but at us. "My dad has another antiques shop he wants to look into tonight. And I don't think it's a good idea for you three to be camping out alone either. Besides, I'm a rotten liar and all, so if your parents asked me to my face, you'd probably get caught, and—"

I heard a cry, and put up a hand to stop Gavin. "Listen!" It sounded again. *Not human. Animal.*

I glanced at Hawke's canoe, but they were way past us now, paddling in the other direction. The sound came from the beaver hut at the end of the lake.

"There it is again," I said.

"I heard it," Packrat said, raising his binoculars. "Can't quite make out what it is, though. There's something there . . . rolling around—"

"Let's go," Roy said, as we all reeled in our lines.

Roy threw us a rope and started his motor. We all knew it would be faster if he towed us. I thought for sure that the roar of his motor would scare the animal off, but it didn't. He cut it and we listened as we floated toward the struggling animal on the ground. A bird. A large bird of some kind. I knew that call, but I couldn't quite place it.

It raised its white head out from under a dark brown wing.

"The eagle!" I cried, then clamped a hand over my mouth before I scared it even more.

The eagle flapped its wings, beating them against the ground, but it didn't take off. Something was holding it back.

"It's caught," Gavin whispered.

Duh, I thought to myself.

We paddled softly, slowly, forward. The eagle beat its wings against the ground again.

Behind and underneath it, I saw another brown animal and a flash of dull silver. "A second eagle?" I asked. "No, wait." The eagle moved a wing just enough for me to see the animal on the ground better. "A beaver?"

The eagle pecked at something silver by its yellow talon.

A trap! The eagle was caught in a beaver trap!

Chapter 17

An eagle's talons are long and razor-sharp, easily cutting through to the bone anything it comes in contact with.

The eagle lay with its wings spread open on the ground. It kept pecking at its talon in the trap.

Down and away from the bird, we slowly coasted in to the shore, trying hard not to make any sudden moves. It wasn't easy, though. The eagle kept its yellow eyes on our every move.

"Shouldn't we call someone?" Packrat asked.

"The eagle might break its leg by the time they could get here," I said.

Gavin agreed. "Or it might die of fright."

When the boats hit shore, we took turns, one by one, stepping out and pulling them onto land. As the four of us started to move toward the eagle, it thrashed around on the ground like crazy. We took several steps backward and crouched as low to the ground as we could.

Looking at its sharp, hooked, yellow beak, I took a deep breath. "Maybe only I should go."

"I can do it if you want," Gavin said.

"My eagles. My rescue."

He nodded. "You know what to do?"

I asked for Packrat's coat, keeping my eyes on the eagle as I answered Gavin. "I've saved animals from traps before." I didn't tell him an eagle would be a first.

I took little steps, creeping closer and closer. The eagle beat its wings against the ground. Mouth open, it shrieked. But its eyes looked panicked. Sad.

I crouched down so I wouldn't look like a big mountain lion hunting prey. "It's okay," I said as soothingly as I could. "I'm here to help."

"Any signs of blood?" Gavin asked.

I tried to see past the eagle, to its talon in the trap. "Not yet."

"That's good," Roy said.

Packrat spoke up. "I just looked it up on my phone. That's a spring-loaded trap."

"Got it." Still crouched, I was now about six feet from it. I could see the black pupils in its yellow eyes, as well as every single feather, including the one brown feather on the back of the head. It was the mom eagle.

I'd read that she was two and a half feet long, with a wingspan of six feet, but crouched next to her in real life, she was so much bigger than I'd dreamed. She could easily slice my skin with her beak and talons. I hesitated.

But she was in trouble. And she had four chicks at home in her nest, depending on her. On me.

I slowly stood, holding the coat out in front of me. The eagle struggled to be free again. "Don't be scared," I whispered. Although I wasn't sure who was shaking more, me or her.

I tossed Packrat's coat over her.

Just as I'd hoped, the eagle went still when she couldn't see. I signaled to the others with a finger to my lips, then motioned for them to come forward. Each one of them held down a corner of Packrat's coat while I turned back the corner covering the steel trap.

"Ewww!" I hissed, putting a hand to my nose. In the trap with the eagle's talon was a huge beaver. It was dead, flies buzzing around it. The claws of the trap were tight against its body.

The eagle moved a little and we all went still.

Gavin stretched his neck to see what I was looking at. His brows came together in a frown as he looked around.

The eagle's yellow talon was caught between the beaver and the edge of the trap. The sharp, black, nail-like ends shuddered every few seconds. I resisted the urge to reach out and see just how sharp one was.

There was no blood—only a scratch on the leg above the talon. Her "toes" were wiggling, so nothing seemed broken. "You're one lucky duck," I whispered. When the eagle thrashed, I chuckled a little. "Okay, okay, one lucky eagle."

I studied the trap until I found the release lever. Not wanting to put my hand in there, I grabbed hold of a nearby stick to press on it. "Okay," I said, in as quiet and calm a voice as I could, "on three, I'm going to open the trap. Gavin, you pull off the coat."

"Cover your faces until she's clear," Gavin said.

"Thanks for the warning," Roy said.

"Got it," Packrat agreed.

Why hadn't I thought to warn my friends?

I put one end of the stick on the release lever and counted: "One, two, three . . . go!" The trap sprung open with a sharp click that echoed across the lake. Gavin lifted the coat and they all turned to bury their heads into their arms.

Not me, though. I had to watch.

Everything happened in slow motion.

The coat flew up, opening as the air filled it, then drifted sideways. The eagle raised its head toward the sun, then turned to look my way. Her yellow eye made contact with my green one. She blinked once and flapped her wings once, as if testing them out. Then she flapped her wings again, more quickly this time, and she was airborne! Rising higher and higher, she perched on a nearby branch where, breathing heavily, she stared down at the four of us.

"Whoa," Packrat said, peeking out from under an arm.

Lowering her head to her injured foot, the eagle poked and preened. Then, silently, she lifted off into the air toward her nest across the lake.

"That was a close call," I said.

"Who'd put a trap here?" Roy looked mad—so mad, I was glad the trapper wasn't standing in front of us at this very minute.

"It looked kind of like the beaver got caught first, then the eagle came down to feed, but its leg fell down between the beaver and the trap arms," Gavin said.

"Or the beaver was put here as bait and someone hoped to catch an eagle in it," I said, looking straight at Gavin. Testing him.

Gavin looked down at the trap. "I suppose that's possible."

Possible? Yes, it was very possible. Could someone be hunting eagles?

Chapter 18

An eagle hatchling only weighs three ounces, and is just four to five inches long.

Back at the campground, it was time for Maxwell Moose to hang out with the little kids again. I tiptoed around the corner of the store toward the fire circle and waited for one of the kids to notice me. Sure enough, I heard, "There he is! There's Maxwell!" Several more little campers called out to me, while a few ran over to give me a hug.

"Come see the fire!"

"Where've you been all day! I've been looking for you."

"Do you have a mom and dad?"

"Where do you sleep?"

Packrat did his best to answer all their questions, because Maxwell didn't talk. We decided it wasn't a good idea, just in case there was 1 time when I couldn't do it, and someone else had to take my place.

Dad shook the popcorn popper over the campfire. Families hung out together, chatting and comparing notes about their day, while the kids either came to see me or chased each other. I wandered around patting a head here, giving a noogie there, and basically getting as many laughs as I could.

"Whoa!" Dad scolded the little kids gently. "No running around the fire! Who wants popcorn?"

Lots of hands went up. Adults and kids yelled, "Me!"

"Me! I want popcorn!" Mikey. And Moose!

"Well, come and sit then!" Dad said to everyone. " And I'll tell you a scary story about a ghost who haunts our driveway."

Hawke walked over to stand by the goons. He smiled at each of them, and they chatted like old friends. I couldn't hear what they were saying over the kids' squeals. A few kids still hung on me, chatting and tugging at me to go see their parents. One kid kept pulling my tail. I tried to get Packrat's attention so he could go over and listen in, but he was helping to hand out the popcorn.

I picked up the tail-puller by the armpits to twirl him until I faced those four creeps head-on. *Four?* Now Gavin was with them!

Putting tail-puller down, I gave him a noogie while peeking out of my costume's mouth slot. Moose's head was nodding so quickly his cheeks bounced. He pointed back and forth between himself and Mikey. Mikey rolled his eyes and hit Moose in the arm. Gavin nodded solemnly. His dad joined the group.

I didn't like it. Not at all.

Tail-puller tried to get behind me again, figuring that was the way he'd get twirled. I put my hand on his forehead so he couldn't move toward me. Arms waving, feet trying to step, he giggled. His parents just kept taking photo after photo after photo.

Gavin and his dad walked away.

I picked the kid up with one arm and held him like a football. Then I put my other hand out and charged through the crowd until I was close to the goons, but not so close that they'd stop talking. I set the kid down as his parents rushed over to take more photos.

Packrat looked my way from the campfire and I put up my hand to tell him to stay there. I didn't want Packrat being close to me, to tip them off.

Tail-puller's parents were trying to convince him to get some popcorn before it was all gone. A shy kid, maybe a kindergartner, was inched forward by her parents. I scooched down to her level and waited without moving.

"If you're sure," Mikey said from behind me. "There's no going back once we do it."

Hawke said, "I'm sure. As soon as you know when, let me know."

Their voices got lower, and then I heard them leave. The little girl was an arm's length away. I wanted to jump up, grab Packrat, and yell, "I found the boss!" But this little girl with her big eyes staring straight into Maxwell's kept me rooted in my spot.

Her mom gently said, "Isn't he cute, Mary?"

Mary shook her head. One pointer finger went into her mouth.

Mary's mom kissed me on the nose. "But he's so gentle."

Mary leaned into her mom. "He don't blink. Why don't he blink!"

Another adult crouched down next to Mary. "Because he has special, magical eyes." I looked up, only to see Hawke.

Mary's eyes turned curious. "Magical?"

Hawke nodded solemnly. "His eyes can tell if you have a good heart or a . . . not-so-good heart. Look. Look closely."

Mary stared at me. I stayed very, very still. She blinked once. Twice. "Do I have a good heart?"

Putting my hands together, I made a heart sign as well as I could with my moosy mittens and nodded.

Mary giggled, leaning back into her mom. She didn't look quite so scared now.

But I was. Scared for my eaglets.

Chapter 19

Eagles sharpen their beaks and remove food from them by feaking—rubbing them back and forth along a strong tree branch or stone.

"No," Mom said. "You can't camp out at the Wentworths', and that's final."

Roy had texted that he'd gotten permission. No surprise there. He was at his site, grabbing his sleepover stuff. He said he'd meet us at the store. I thought maybe the rule of two or three would work with Mom, and then we could use her permission to get Packrat's mom's permission.

I was wrong.

"But why?" I cried.

"That's all the way over on the other side of the lake! What if you hurt yourself or somebody tried to steal you?" Mom stopped to ring up a bag of chips and a soda for a customer.

"*Mom!*" I rolled my eyes toward Packrat, then back to Mom with a don't-embarrass-me-in-front-of-my-friend look.

"Well, you asked," she said.

"What if I called you on the radio every hour?"

"No."

"Every half-hour?"

She smiled at the next customer as she rang up their ketchup and hot dogs and rolls, made change, and bagged them, talking to me the whole time. "All night long? Neither you nor I would get any sleep."

Sleeping wasn't part of the plan, but I wasn't telling her that.

"I could just hit the feedback button really quick so you knew I was still alive. You wouldn't even have to answer me."

"No."

A guy dropped some graham crackers, marshmallows, and chocolate bars on the counter. Mom started pushing register keys again.

"Mom! C'mon!" I draped myself over the counter. "Pleeeeeeeease?"

Mom didn't even look my way. I wasn't sure if it was because she didn't believe in ignoring customers, or if she was trying to ignore me.

"You know," I said, "you have no problem letting me hang out in the middle of our ginormous campground all day, with hundreds of strangers from all over the world, but you won't let me go camp on the Wentworths' lawn with the two kids you know best."

The customer chuckled. "Kid's got a point."

He was now my favorite camper in the whole campground. The whole world! Even if I didn't know his name. I moved a little closer to the guy and looked at Mom hopefully. "You do like to say the customer is always right."

"Hey! No ganging up on me in my own store!" Mom let out a huge I'm-about-to-back-down-and-give-him-what-he-wants sigh. Packrat and I leaned in a little closer toward her. She opened her mouth.

The screen door slammed shut behind Packrat's mom and Lucy. Stacey's eyebrows went up, and a smile lit her face. "Hey! What's going on here—and how come we weren't invited?"

Mom said, "I was just about to *reluctantly* let—"

The screen door opened and slammed shut behind the goons. "Hey!" Moose said. "Is there a party and we weren't invited?"

The customer, Stacey, Lucy, my mom, and the goons all chuckled. Packrat and I did not.

"Lucy and I were headed out to pick up a few things at the grocery store," Stacey said. "Do you need anything, Joan?"

"A new brain?" Mom said, letting out another long sigh. Her shoulders slumped as she turned my way. I felt bad for a second, because I knew I had her convinced, even though she was second-guessing her mom radar, which told her not to let me go. Finally, she said, "I guess it'll be okay with me, if it's okay with Stacey."

The goons looked on with interest. Mikey raised an eyebrow.

Uh-oh. Packrat and I exchanged a what-do-we-do-now look. Mom would have to tell Packrat's mom what we wanted to do in front of—

The screen door slammed shut again. When all eyes turned toward him, Hawke stopped to put his hands in his back pockets. He gave a small grin, then opened his mouth.

"No, you weren't invited!" I said, throwing my hands in the air.

"Cooper!" Mom exclaimed.

Everyone chuckled except Packrat and me. This was getting ridiculous!

Mom looked back at Stacey. "The kids want to—"

Packrat stepped between them and said quickly, "—camp out on my site."

Mom frowned. "That's not—"

"Yes it is," I said, knowing exactly what my friend was doing. The goons . . . Hawke . . . we couldn't tell them we were planning to stake out the eagles' nest. Then it wouldn't be a stakeout. "Sleeping at Packrat's. It's exactly what we want to do."

Packrat's mom smiled. "Of course, it's okay. It's always okay."

I tried not to sigh out loud. Good thing those goons were dumb.

Mom looked relieved. "Kids! They change their minds like the wind!"

Everyone laughed again. I'm glad *they* were getting such a big kick out of this. *Sheesh.* The customer left, while Hawke strode down a store aisle and the goons bellied up to the self-help coffee counter.

"I need to restock a couple of things in here, if you don't mind picking them up," my mom said to Stacey. "I'm out of marshmallows. Graham crackers too. But I need the plain ones . . ." Mom grabbed a notepad and pencil before heading into the aisles.

Roy burst in with a sleeping bag under one arm and a backpack slung over his shoulder. "Ready to stake——"

I shot him a warning look.

Lucy stepped closer to us. "Stake?"

"A tent on my site," Packrat said.

"But . . . *Oww!*" Roy picked up his foot and shook it, then glared at Packrat.

"I'm sorry, I didn't see it there," he said sweetly.

I sighed. We weren't very good at this spy thing.

Lowering my voice so the goons in the aisle couldn't hear me, I said, "We were gonna camp out by the lake, but Mom wouldn't let me. So Packrat is having us instead."

"Sounds like a good backup plan," Lucy said. "Do you all need anything while we're in town? Chips? Cookies? Hot cocoa?"

Roy spoke up. "How about some——"

Packrat said, "I've got that. We're good. And we're all pretty tired from working all day. I think we'll be going to sleep early, right after a quick game of Monopoly."

Packrat obviously had a plan. I nodded. Packrat yawned. Roy looked from Packrat, to me. "You're all party poopers!"

I heard Moose, at the back of the store, snicker. Then I heard Mikey smack him in the arm.

"But Mikey, he said *pooper.*"

Lucy quickly looked their way, then did an I-can't-believe-they're-grown-men shake of her head. When she looked back at us, she had a small frown on her face.

"Are those guys still bothering you?" she asked.

I thought of a half-truth. "No. They finally get it—that we don't have their geocache box. But I promised to . . . to keep an eye out for it."

"Good," she said.

Chapter 20

Adult bald eagles have very few natural enemies. Some of their greatest threats come from human causes, such as illegal hunting, habitat loss, and electrocution from power lines and wind turbines.

"I'm dead if my mom finds out," I said, dropping my sleeping bag on the dew-wet grass under the starry sky.

"Me too," Packrat said.

"I'm safe," Roy said. He'd laid his rolled-up sleeping bag next to the rock wall to lean against it. Hands behind his head, he stared up at the stars with a huge goofy grin. "I gotta admit, Packrat, I didn't think you had it in you to fib like that! And not just *fib.*" Roy sat up to look him square in the eye. "You flat-out lied! A decoy tent . . . snoring noises . . . lights flicking on and off on a timer. You're a genius!"

We'd staked out this spot along the rock wall, under the trees where it was darkest, but where we could easily see the eagles' nest. Hoping *we'd* be hard to see from the water, the only stuff we'd brought with us were our sleeping bags and snacks, hoping to fade away into the shadows.

Packrat pulled a flashlight from his pocket and pointed the light at the ground.

"No light," I said, putting a hand over it. "If the goons are headed this way, they'll see it."

He shut it off. "How do you think they'll come—boat or trail?"

Roy said, "Boat. It's quieter. Faster."

"Land," I said. "They drive over, hike in. Harder to see them."

My eyes had adjusted enough to the dark, and now I could see the eagles' nest high in the tree. Or the shadow of it, really, since it blocked out the stars behind it. One adult eagle perched on its edge. I wasn't sure which, since I couldn't see its markings clearly. Suddenly, it tilted its head to look down on us with one eye.

I held my breath. How king-like it was. This was the closest I'd ever been to the nest while there were eaglets in it. I was glad that it didn't fly away or cry out or anything.

Roy hooked his thumb over his shoulder to point to the woods on the other side of the wall. "No matter how they come, they'll probably make their way to the nest from over there, since the tree is on that side. If we stay low, we'll hear them before they see us. We can take 'em! Packrat—you got the rope I gave you? So we can tie them up?"

Chirp, chirp, chirp came from above us. Four light-gray heads poked up out of the nest. Then there were three. Then four again. One of them used its beak to pull itself across to its parent, who poked and pulled at the grasses around them, then looked upward toward the sky. All four eaglets started fussing in earnest.

We three leaned against the rough, cool wall. Packrat unfolded his tabletop telescope and we took turns looking through it at satellites and stars and constellations.

"There's Orion's Belt," I said.

"Where?" asked Packrat.

I automatically reached for my flashlight to point out the three stars sitting low in the sky, then remembered our no-flashlight rule. I leaned over next to him so he could look down my arm to where my finger pointed. "Across there."

"There's the Big Dipper, and Little Dipper," Roy said.

"Those are easy. Saturn's over there."

Packrat pointed upward, but before he could say anything, Roy put a hand over his mouth. "*Shhhhhh!*"

Crunch.

Something or someone had stepped on crunchy, dried-up leaves. Two seconds of silence, then *crunch, crunch, crunch.* Then silence.

We crouched behind the wall.

"Can you see anything?" Packrat whispered my way.

I shook my head.

"I'm ready!" Roy said.

Packrat tapped my arm to offer me something. Binoculars? I raised my eyebrows. He smiled.

I put them to my eyes. Night-vision goggles. Yes!

Crunch. Crunch. Crunch.

I had both elbows on the wall, scanning the woods beyond. Roy looked ready to leap over it in a single bound.

Crunch, crunch, snap!

There! I saw it! A hundred yards away, moving slowly toward us on four legs, was a masked animal. It stopped every few feet to bury its nose under dead leaves as it searched for plants, fruits, insects, or maybe a mouse to eat.

I chuckled. "Raccoon."

Everyone sighed. The eagle adults looked down as if to say *Suckers*. One of the adults spread its wings and lifted off the nest.

Roy yawned.

The raccoon waddled forward. It stopped, then stood on its hind legs to look up at the nest.

That was weird. Keeping my eyes on the raccoon, I heard Roy yawn a second time. "Take a nap," I told him. "I'll be okay."

"No way," Roy said. "I'm getting a second wind here; I can pull an all-nighter with you two."

"I'm a night owl," Packrat said. "I'm not ready to sleep yet."

The raccoon went back on all fours, moved forward for a minute, then stood. It wiggled its nose in the air, first to the left, then to the right.

"What are you looking at?" I wondered aloud.

Roy and Packrat crawled over to look. The raccoon had made his way to the eagles' tree and stood with his paws on it, looking up again.

Roy frowned. "Do you think he knows what's up there?"

"Raccoons eat eggs," Packrat said.

"But the nest is fifty feet up. And there aren't any eggs . . ." Roy's voice trailed off.

"Raccoons—" I didn't get to finish my sentence, because the raccoon had started to climb.

Roy and Packrat cried out at the same time. I jumped up and over the wall, racing toward the tree. Crunching footsteps behind me told me my friends were right behind. We stopped about five feet from the tree, looking up to find the raccoon already halfway to the top.

The adult eagle looked down, flapped its wings, and gave some very unwelcome, short, high-pitched whistles. The raccoon backed up a bit, and I thought maybe it would come down. But it finished the climb, stopping only when it was directly under the nest. It poked a nose between some branches, which had the adult flapping its wings and poking the nest from above.

The raccoon reached up to tug on a stick. Dry grass fell from the opening it made, slowly floating to the ground.

The other adult eagle swooped around the outside of the nest, giving the same high-pitched calls. This had the raccoon retreating under the nest again. The adult with the chicks flapped its wings, calling over and over again.

The raccoon looked down at us. Then it reached up with one of its fingered hands to pull on another stick. More grass and some small sticks fell.

"Back off!" I warned. "It won't climb down if we're here." I waved my two friends back to the wall.

The eagle in the nest flapped its wings to charge the small hole the raccoon had made. The masked intruder backed down the tree about five feet. The other eagle swooped past the tree once, twice, which had the raccoon scrambling to turn and climb down face-first. It stopped another twenty feet down to perch on a branch, and once again looked up at the nest.

"Is it nuts?" Packrat said.

"Does it *want* to be eaglet food?" Roy asked.

I looked at him, eyebrows raised. "No. It wants the eaglets to be its midnight snack."

"Seriously?" Packrat whistled low.

Roy pointed at the raccoon. Behind it, the eagle silently swooped in, talons down. "Get him!" Roy whispered. "Get him!"

The raccoon must have felt the eagle coming, because at the last second it tried to scramble out of the way. Instead, it fell.

We all gasped. Packrat put his hands to his mouth, while Roy put his hands on his head.

The raccoon got up on all fours, shook itself, and waddled back the way it'd come.

The eagle calmly landed on the nest next to its mate and gave a regal look at the retreating troublemaker, as if to say *And don't come back.*

"That was close," I said.

"You aren't kidding," Packrat added, as the three of us moved away from the nest now that the excitement was over. "Too close!"

"Raccoons going after eaglets. I wouldn't have believed it if I hadn't seen it for myself," Roy said.

I smiled at his back.

We laid out our sleeping bags. The air had gotten cool, so we sat inside them, with all our clothes on.

Packrat opened his coat and pulled out a travel-size game of Sorry. "I'm blue," he said.

"Green." I yawned a long, from-the-stomach yawn.

"Red," Roy said.

Packrat spun the little spinner in the middle. It landed on 1, so he moved a man out onto START. Roy did the same.

"Coming right behind you!" I teased. Five spins later, I still hadn't moved a man out, but Packrat already had his two near home stretch, and Roy had one.

My turn. I spun the little spinner just as Roy said, "I wish Gavin could have come, too."

I quietly said, "I'm glad he didn't. One. Finally!" I moved a man out onto START.

Packrat spun. "Cooper's afraid he's in on it."

"Gavin wouldn't do anything like that!" Roy sat straight up. His eyes shot daggers at us, as one fist clenched the token he'd just taken off START. We shushed him, so his next words were whispers, but just as strong. "He's not that kind of kid."

"Roy, would you think about it?" I pleaded. "His dad is an antiques dealer, so they know about this kind of stuff. Gavin didn't want anything to do with us 'kids' until after he heard about the parts. At the very least, he could rat us out. He and his dad had a long talk with Hawke and the goons today."

"Did you hear what they said?" he asked.

"No. I wasn't close enough."

Packrat moved his man. It landed on me and knocked me home again. "Sorry!"

"No, you're not!" I gave him a little shove to the shoulder, then spun to get a 1, and moved a man out. "I did hear Mikey say something like 'There's no going back once we do it,' to Hawke."

Roy stopped with his hand over the spinner. "Do what?"

I shrugged. "Steal the eaglet? Trade the parts?"

Roy spun a 5 and knocked my man back home again.

"What?" I yelled. "Are you kidding me?"

Roy turned on his flashlight and put it under his chin.
"*Mwaaaaaaaahaaaaaaa!*"

I pushed him over, laughing. Packrat pushed me. Roy vowed revenge. Suddenly, I shushed them both. Roy shut off his flashlight.

They both looked at me, waiting for my reason. But it wasn't anything I had heard or seen; I'd just had a feeling. I moved onto all fours and waited for my eyes to adjust, scanning the lake, until I saw it. Something moving quietly over the water in the distance.

"There!" I said, lying down on the ground. "Something's coming."

Packrat, Roy, and I crawled as low to the ground as we could, as close to the wall as possible. We never took our eyes off the boater.

"I only see one," I whispered. "In the boat."

Packrat fumbled in a pocket for the night-vision goggles. Putting them to his eyes, he gasped. "Not who we thought." He passed them to Roy, who whistled quietly before passing them to me.

It was Hawke.

"Do you think he saw us?" I asked.

Packrat shrugged.

As he got near the nest, we moved even closer to the wall. His canoe slowed. He looked toward the Wentworths' dark house, then turned his head slowly until he seemed to be looking right at us. I wanted so badly to scoot closer to the wall, but I resisted. If I had trouble seeing him, he'd have trouble spotting us. I hoped.

Then Hawke looked up at the eagles.

Both adults were still there, one perched on the edge of the nest, the other on a nearby branch. The eagle on the edge turned its whole body around to face Hawke. It tipped its head down to look at him. They stared at each other for a long time. Then Hawke looked in our direction again, quickly this time, before taking up his paddle and moving silently on.

When he was out of sight, Packrat and I slumped to the ground, giggling a little.

Roy watched Hawke until he was out of sight.

"Whoa. That was close," Packrat said.

"I know. I don't think he saw us, though." I yawned, and gazed back up at the eagles and their rare quadruplets. I was gonna keep them safe no matter what. Safe from raccoons. From eaglet-stealing goons. From bosses who steal eagle parts.

We settled in our bags again. Since we'd messed up the game board with our wrestling, we started from scratch.

The next thing I knew, Gavin was shaking my shoulder, telling me to wake up.

"One of the babies is gone!"

Chapter 21

Fossils from ancient sea eagles suggest they've been around for 25 million years.

"Huh? *What?* What are *you* doing here?" My eyes felt like they had sand in them. My throat was dry, and my shoulders were stiff and sore. I lifted my chin and arched my back to get rid of the aches I'd gotten from leaning against the hard, cool, rock wall.

Looking out across the lake, I realized the sky had gone from black to a deep, early-morning blue. Then I sat up straight as Gavin's words sunk into my sleepy brain. Looking skyward, I saw only three eaglet heads. No adults. How could one of the eagle babies be gone?

"But . . . I only closed my eyes for a *minute!*" I jumped to my feet. Hearing a snore, I looked down to see Packrat curled up against the wall, a little bit of drool forming at the corner of his wide-open mouth. I nudged him with my foot.

When I looked to Roy, who was standing nearby, rubbing his eyes, he said, "Don't ask me. He just woke me up, too."

I shaded my eyes and looked up at the nest. "You miscounted!"

Gavin stood beside me, staring up too. "No. I kept both eyes on the nest as I paddled over here to find you. There's only three."

"Then one fell out! Or . . . or maybe the raccoon doubled back!" I did not want to hear what I knew Gavin was going to say.

"Raccoon?" Gavin looked confused for a second. "No, it wasn't a raccoon, Cooper." He held up a fist full of multicolored rope. One end of it hung down, almost to the ground, swinging back and forth between us. "Raccoons don't use this."

"Where'd you get that?" I grabbed it, realizing right away this wasn't your normal rope. It was thicker and stiffer, more like cord. The stuff for mountain climbing. For any kind of climbing.

120

"It wasn't far from the bottom of the tree. Probably dropped by accident when they were leaving."

"Who?" I cried.

"I don't know!" Gavin's voice rose a bit too. He ran a hand over his face. "Listen, I didn't see anyone but you three when I got here. I didn't pass anyone as I paddled over."

Packrat finally got to his feet. "Wh-what? Who?"

I combed a hand through my hair, trying to clear my head. I remembered a game of Sorry, getting beaten soundly, using my stupid flashlight to make a scary face, Hawke in a canoe. I groaned.

I'd fallen asleep! What the heck kind of staking-out game warden was I, anyway?

Then I remembered. "Hawke paddled by just after one in the morning."

Gavin shook his head. "Hawke? He—"

"Why are you here, anyway?" I turned my anger on Gavin.

Now his eyes narrowed. "If I wasn't, those eaglet thieves would have an even bigger head start."

Packrat stepped up beside me. "You didn't answer his question, Gavin."

"I went by your tent to see if any of you kids wanted to go fishing," Gavin said, ducking his head for a second.

He's lying, I thought.

"I didn't think you heard me call in, what with all the snoring." Gavin gave Packrat a small smile. "Nice job with the fake sleepover, by the way."

"Thanks—" Packrat began.

"So I poked my head in."

"I still don't get why you're here!" I pointed a finger at him.

Roy got between us to point a finger at me. "Hey! What's it matter? Apparently we're pretty heavy sleepers. We woulda slept till noon if he hadn't come to help us! "

Help us? How could Roy still think Gavin wasn't in on this?

"Cooper," Gavin said, putting a hand on my shoulder, "you can't keep getting mixed up in all this stuff. You're going to get in trouble—or worse!"

I shook off his hand. "We need to go back," I cut him off. "Back to the campground." I didn't want to know what *he* thought. This was my investigation. My campground. My eagles!

And my fault.

Roy, Packrat, and Gavin gathered our supplies and our sleeping bags while I took a look under the tree. Lots of footprints, including the raccoon's. Most of the boot prints were huge, but there was one set of smaller prints, a little bigger than mine.

I went back, grabbed my sleeping bag off the ground, and threw it over my shoulder. "We have to stop them from leaving with that eaglet!"

"But who?" Packrat asked. "The goons? Hawke?"

"I'm not sure," I said, studying the rope that was still in my hands. Could those clumsy goons have climbed the tree to get the eaglet? And silently, so silently that we slept through it? Hawke certainly could have. I looked at Gavin's feet. Or did they have help from someone else?

We hauled our sleeping bags to the canoes, tossed them in, and climbed in over them. Packrat and I took one canoe, and Roy joined Gavin in his.

When we'd paddled away from shore, Packrat asked, "How long ago do you think they were here? We might be too late."

Inside, I stormed. *How could I mess up this badly?* All the frustration of the last few minutes came out in a rush. I raised my canoe paddle and slapped it down on the water. Then I sighed.

Packrat stopped paddling and turned in his seat. "What if I called Aunt Lucy? She could check the site . . . To see if they've left? She did say to call if we needed help."

We all went silent. Calling Aunt Lucy meant two things. One: She'd know those snores coming from Packrat's tent all night weren't us; and two: Packrat and I might as well forget about setting foot anywhere outside the campground for the rest of the summer.

But the eagles were more important than our getting in trouble.

"I guess. Yeah. Go ahead."

Before Packrat could dial any numbers, though, his phone rang. Looking at it, he groaned.

"Busted."

He hit the ANSWER button, but didn't have to say a word. A voice came through immediately. He put it on speaker and held out the phone between us so I could hear too. It was Aunt Lucy.

"I went out to bring you boys hot cocoa. You're not in the tent!"

"I know. We—"

"Where are you?"

"On the lake."

"Who are you with?" Her voice was very sharp.

"Cooper, Gavin, Roy."

"How long have you been out there?"

"Welllll . . . " Packrat hesitated.

Aunt Lucy's voice cracked with indignation as she connected the dots herself. "You've been out there *all night,* haven't you?" Silence, then, "Why?"

Packrat and I looked at each other. *Why?* Not, *What do you think you're doing?* or, *You're too young to be out on the lake by yourselves at night?* or even, *How dare you take off in the middle of the night and not tell anybody?*

I said, "Well, we thought—"

"This has something to do with those two men, doesn't it?"

"*Aunt Lucy!*" Packrat had finally had enough. "Listen!"

There was a harrumph, then a sharp, but quieter "I'm listening."

At Packrat's yell, Roy and Gavin had turned around to look. I saw Roy point back at us with his paddle. Gavin nodded, and they turned their canoe around.

Packrat looked at me and raised his eyebrows with an are-you-sure? look.

I was gonna be in so much trouble, but I mouthed back *Go ahead* to him. It was the only chance the baby eagle had.

So he told her about how Mikey and Moose had mentioned taking one of the eaglets off its parents' hands. How we'd hatched the plan to stake out the nest. How we'd fallen asleep and . . . then he mentioned one was gone.

Aunt Lucy didn't skip a beat. "Did you see anything?"

"Nah. All we found was a rope at the bottom of the tree. That's how we knew someone had been there."

She said something that sounded like it could have been a swear word. "Cooper, did you tell your parents?"

"Do we have to?" Packrat pleaded. "You said that if they bothered us, we could come to you!"

"But you didn't come to me *before* you snuck out by yourselves onto the lake in the middle of the night. I could get into as much trouble with your mother as you, if—"

Suddenly, we heard another voice. A younger, squeakier voice. *Molly!*

I slapped a hand to my forehead as Packrat doubled over to put his head on his knees. There were murmured voices; Molly's had question marks all over them, and Aunt Lucy's were soothing. Hope rose in me like an eagle soaring on a windy day. I could almost see her turning Molly around and gently pushing her toward home with a good explanation.

"Well, that does it," she said with a sigh. "I'm in as deep as you now. I fibbed for you. Get home immediately. I hope you've had a good time fishing early, early, early this morning."

"Thanks, Aunt Lucy!"

"You're the best!" I added.

"We're coming!" Roy dipped a paddle in the water.

Gavin was weirdly quiet, staring back toward the eagles' nest.

"See you in a minute," she said.

"Aunt Lucy!" Packrat said quickly. "I almost forgot. Can you check on the goo—I mean, Mikey and Moose? Don't let them leave if you can help it, okay?"

She sighed. "Leave it to me. But you owe me, big-time. And I will collect, young man."

Chapter 22

Eagle chicks are mostly fed fish. They snatch it whole from their parents' beaks, eating as much as they can in a single feeding.

An eagle cried from somewhere behind us. I looked back. It was circling the trees around its nest. I don't know about the others guys, but I dug my paddle a little lower in the water and pulled it back toward me a little faster. We had to get back to find the baby eaglet before something happened to it.

Or before those goons left the campground with it.

Hearing another chatter call from the eagle, Roy said, "It's still looking for its chick."

I paused, paddle half in, half out of the water. "What if those guys don't know what to feed it? It could starve!"

I heard Packrat keeping time with me. Roy and Gavin were just ahead and to our right. Gavin stopped paddling to look back.

"Actually," he said, "they can go for days without food if they have to."

"No, they can't," I insisted. "The parents feed them every few hours. I've watched."

We had floated up beside their canoe. Gavin shook his head and dipped his paddle into the water. "No, they have crops. It's a pouch that stores food—"

"I know what a crop is!" I said. I dug my paddle in and pushed at the water with everything I had to move ahead of their canoe. Still, I felt like Packrat and Roy's eyes were on me.

I knew what a crop was. But I hadn't known that eagles have them. *How did I not know that?*

The other three talked all the way back, paddles dipping in the water over and over. But I didn't hear a word. I couldn't stop the thoughts whirling around in my brain. Gavin knew a ton about eagles. More than me, even. Gavin was there, rope in hand, this morning. Gavin didn't want to come with us to stake out the eagles because he had something important to do with his dad.

Did we have it all wrong? Were Mr. Valley and Gavin the buyers? Or was his dad the boss? Was Gavin sent to keep an eye on us?

I looked sideways at him. He didn't look like an eagle killer. He looked as worried as Packrat, Roy, or me.

Maybe he was worried about getting caught by us.

Roy wouldn't like that very much.

We reached the campground beach and pulled our canoes up to the dock. We quickly locked them up, grabbed our life vests, paddles, and sleeping bags, and jogged toward Packrat's site.

I thought for sure we'd find all our moms standing by Packrat's tent, tapping their feet, hands on hips, ground-ation on their lips. Because even Roy's mom would be mad that he'd gone camping with us when we didn't have permission from our moms.

But no one was there. The only sounds we heard were the fake snores coming from the tent.

"Weird," Packrat whispered. "Where's Aunt Lucy?"

"You asked her to keep an eye on the goons. Maybe she went over to their site," I suggested.

The four of us walked as quietly as we could so as not to wake up any curious campers. A group of kids walking around at this time of the morning would have some adults thinking the worst of us. Of course, they wouldn't exactly be wrong. We stuck to the playground, so we didn't run into anyone on the way.

I didn't realize I was holding my breath—for fear the goons had pulled out already with the eaglet—until we'd rounded the corner and could see that their motor home was on the site. There was still a chance we could get this little one back to its parents!

Unless we had the wrong thieves, said a little voice inside my head. I told it to shut up.

We crouched down behind a small grouping of young birch trees. Packrat parted the branches with his hands to get a better look at the motor home. "Do you think they're in there?"

"I don't see any lights. No one's moving around," Gavin said.

He had a good point. Trailers and motor homes rocked back and forth a little whenever someone moved around in them. We all watched for a couple of minutes, but it still didn't look like anyone was in there.

"They could have easily made it back, dumped the eaglet, and left again," Roy said. "Only one way to find out." He stood up, rubbing his hands on his pants as he eyed the motor home.

I grabbed the back of his sweatshirt and pulled him back down. "I'm going. Alone."

"Hey! How come you get to have all the fun?"

"Because if anyone catches me, I can say my dad asked me to . . . to . . . get his tool or something. If all of us are going in, it'll look more suspicious."

Packrat nodded. "I gotta admit, that's a foolproof plan," he said. "Any camper here would believe it."

A low rumbling sound had Gavin, Packrat, and me looking at each other with round eyes. Roy put a hand to his stomach. "Hurry up, okay? I'm starving." His stomach rumbled again.

Packrat took a package of blueberry Pop-Tarts out of one of his coat pockets. "Your stomach will get us killed. Eat these."

Roy dug in. I have no idea how he could eat at a time like this.

"You guys be lookouts, okay?" I asked.

"Whoa, whoa, whoa . . . whoa." Gavin's eyes were huge, and he put a hand out like he was going to stop me. "You can't just walk into their motor home. That's not a legal search."

Roy spoke with a mouthful. "It's on his prop-er-ty."

Packrat nodded. "And it's a life-or-death situation."

I smiled. My friends were backing me up. Gavin looked at the three of us in disbelief. When he realized we were serious, he held up his hands like he was surrendering.

The sun was still rising behind the trees, so it was light enough that we had to be careful not to be seen. And there was the early-morning quietness to deal with. One snapping twig, and a neighboring camper would be jumping out of bed to look out the window.

I stared at the motor home. It seemed so much farther to the door than it had a minute ago.

"Cooper," Packrat whispered, "you got this. You're the Manhunt king."

Bending my knees a bit to lower my height, and scanning every inch of ground before taking a step, I slowly crept forward until I was standing behind the motor home. I stopped to listen for cars driving through, people inside or out, and eaglet cries.

Hearing nothing, I rounded the corner of the motor home and stood with my back against it. I kept it there as I moved sideways toward the door at the other end. Ten steps to go. Eight. Seven.

Headlights!

I dropped to the ground and rolled into the dark underneath. *Crack!* I saw stars. Pain shot through my head, and I realized I'd hit it on a pipe running along the bottom of the motor home. I rubbed the sore spot. "*Oww!*" Glancing back, I saw Packrat, Roy, and Gavin duck out of sight.

It seemed like forever before the car rolled into view. It was still dark enough out that I couldn't make out what kind of car, or the color, but when it rolled on by, I knew we were safe.

I slid on my stomach until I was out. Roy, Packrat, and Gavin popped their heads back up again. Packrat gave me a thumbs-up. I brushed off the dirt from my shirt and jeans.

Six steps to go.

Five.

A light went on in the front of the trailer next door. I crouched down low to the ground. All the windows had their curtains drawn, so I couldn't see in. Had they heard me? Inside the trailer, footsteps padded from the front to the back. I heard murmured voices; a mom and her kid, maybe? The footsteps went back to the front and the light went off.

I stood again, but this time I moved more quickly toward the door. I peeked up and down the road and, seeing no one, stood on the first step and pulled the door lever out.

I'm not sure who was more surprised, me or my friends, when the door actually pulled open. I quickly looked their way. Roy made motions to go inside already. Gavin made a slicing motion across his neck. It didn't take an interpreter to know he meant *Abort the mission*. Packrat shrugged his shoulders.

I ducked inside and gently shut the door behind me.

This was one of those fancy motor homes. Everything was gold and white and shiny and brand-new. To the right of the door was a cockpit of sorts—all window from just behind the driver's seat, all the way around to just behind the passenger seat. The dash was littered with maps and papers. The console between the two huge, recliner-ish chairs held two old Styrofoam coffee cups. A fly walked along the edge of one.

To the left was the kitchen and living room. I took a step forward, then realized my dirty sneakers might leave marks that would give away that I'd been here. I took them off and set them to the right, just under the curtain that divided the passenger seat from the rest of the motor home.

I tiptoed to a door on the left-hand side. I slowly opened it, hoping to find our eaglet in the bathtub–shower stall combination. But no such luck. That would have been too easy, for sure.

I was backing out of there to open the door to the bedroom when I heard car tires *pop-pop-popping* softly on the dirt road. I froze.

This one will drive by, too, I thought. *What were the chances?*

The car slowed. Those tire pops sounded right outside the motor home!

I ran toward the door, then realized they were parked right outside it.

I was trapped!

I ran to the back of the motor home, into the bedroom, looking frantically for a way out. But there was none, because motor homes don't have back doors. *I knew that! What was I thinking?* I wasn't thinking. *That* was the problem.

My heart was racing so fast, everything seemed out of focus. I was breathing like I'd just finished a marathon. Hearing one car door open, I took a deep, deep breath. Tried to calm down.

Think, think, think.

Then I saw it. The little red sign next to the right side window.

FOR EMERGENCY EXIT ONLY——PULL LEVER FORWARD.

I heard the second door open and voices talking. I even heard the campers one site over shushing them. In seconds, I had pulled that lever forward, popped the window out, and shimmied through to drop on the ground beside the back corner of the motor home. It was too high up for me to close the window again, but at least I was out!

I got as low to the ground as I could and moved quickly to the back corner of the motor home. Roy's head was barely up over the hedge. He held up a hand to stop me, then ducked back down. The motor home rocked slightly as the door opened and the heavy goons stepped inside, one by one. Roy, Packrat, and Gavin's heads all popped up at the same time as they frantically waved me forward. I cleared the brush and dropped to the ground, breathing heavily, trying to catch my breath.

"That was cool!" Packrat whispered. He had a huge grin on his face. "You were awesome!"

I smiled back, one hand over my stomach, which wasn't feeling so good. Not that I'd tell them that.

"No eaglet?" Gavin didn't sound surprised.

I shook my head. Still gasping, I wasn't quite ready to talk.

Roy looked at my feet and frowned.

My stomach rolled again.

I'd left my shoes inside the motor home.

Chapter 23

Eagles have three toes that point forward and one toe that points backward.

We all knew the exact minute my sneakers were found. The motor home rocked from side to side like crazy. Heavy footsteps were heard, and cupboard doors banged open and closed as they pounded around, looking for me. They got another shushing from the family on the other side.

Finally, Moose tried to put his head out the open window, but he got it stuck, so he called Mikey, which had the campers on both sides shushing.

Mikey pushed inward on both sides of Moose's head until he could pull him back. We saw the motor home rock back and forth again as the two of them raced from the back to the front. Moose fell out the door, and Mikey landed on top of him on the ground, in a heap.

When they'd untangled themselves, Mikey stormed to the back corner of the motor home. He whispered, "I know you're out there, kid." He held up my sneakers.

Roy started to stand, but I frowned at him. I signaled my friends to stay low, that I had this. They all shook their heads.

I pointed to myself and then pointed up.

They stared me down in an if-you-go-we-all-go kind of way. So we stood up together.

I held out my hands. "You got us."

The goons took a step forward. I whispered, "Stay there or I'll yell." I pointed at the trailers either side of us.

The sun had moved just above the tree line, and there was no mistaking how angry those big, square faces were as they glared at us.

Mikey tossed me my sneakers. "I know what you're looking for. It ain't here."

"Where—?" I began.

He cut me off. "The boss wants us to trade ya: the box for the baby bird."

"Eaglet," Gavin corrected him.

"But I thought it was a chick," Moose said.

"Shut up," Mikey hissed at him. To me, he said, "Whaddya say?"

"I don't have it," I said.

One side of Mikey's mouth curved upward in a smile. He reached into his back pocket and pulled out the photo he'd found on the bathroom floor. "Yes, you do."

Mikey moved forward. I looked at the trailers on either side of their motor home and opened my mouth, but he smiled even more. "You won't yell. You're in this as deep as I am. All this time I was worried you'd go running to your parents, but now I know you don't want *them* to know about any of *this*." He slapped the photo with the back of his big hand. " 'Cause if they find out, they'll shut down your little geocaching operation. Am I right? We can keep them out of it. Just bring me the box."

"I don't—"

Mikey thrust the picture at me over the brush.

"It's not mine," I insisted, even as my hand shook taking it.

Mikey's grin got larger. "The boss was right." With his pointer finger, he poked me in the chest, right in the middle of the born to camp at logo, like it was a giant bull's-eye.

"So?" I tried not to show how fast my heart was racing. "Lots of campers have this sweatshirt. We sell it in the—"

Mikey grabbed my forearm to hold my wrist up between us. On it was my blue-and-black survival bracelet. In his other hand, he waved the photo: same hand, same bracelet, holding the eagle claw.

"Bring me the box," he demanded.

I thought fast. It was no use pretending anymore. "It's going to take an hour to get it, easy."

When Mikey's eyebrows went down, I said quickly, "It's hidden. Across the lake."

He smiled again. "Well, then, just give us the coordinates."

"You can't get to it," Roy said, crossing his arms in front of his chest.

"Yeah," Packrat spoke up. "It's in that canyon."

I need to buy us some time, I thought. *Maybe there's still a chance to help the eaglet.*

"There's no way into it for you guys unless you rappel down or jump down the waterfall."

Moose shuffled from one foot to the other. "I don't want to rappel or jump," he whined.

Mikey didn't look too sure about doing it either. "Fine. Give us the closest coordinates you've got, and we'll meet you there."

"Even trade?" I asked.

He grinned again. "Even trade. Your box for the eaglet."

"Where is it?" I asked, putting my hands out. "Don't hurt it, please."

"It's safe with—" began Moose.

"None of your business!" Mikey interrupted.

Shushes came from the neighboring campers again.

"Half an hour," he said. "No more. Or I won't be responsible for what happens to that chick."

Chapter 24

Eaglets are born with brown eyes and a brown beak.
The eyes and beak don't turn yellow until sometime
during the eaglet's fourth year.

We paddled directly across the lake for the second time that morning, taking kayaks this time. The sun was directly above the trees now, and it was hot. The lake was calm. The air, heavy. We pulled up alongside a birch tree that had grown straight over the water's surface. One by one, we got out of the kayaks and pulled them onto shore, hiding them under bushes so they couldn't be seen from the lake.

Packrat dug out the hiking GPS and turned it on. Silently, we all walked in the direction of our canyon.

I stole glances at Gavin. He hadn't said more than two words in a row since I'd gotten caught by the goons. I could tell he hadn't wanted to come, but we kind of made him. I talked him into it because I wanted to keep him in my sights. Roy pleaded with him because he thought we could use the extra hands.

What Roy and Packrat didn't know was that I had looked back after we'd first climbed into the kayaks and started paddling, and there was Gavin, texting on his phone.

I glared until he looked up. He held it up. "Just my dad. I have to check in every so often or he'll get mad."

Right.

It didn't take long before we heard the babbling brook. We crossed it, only stepping on the gray, dry rocks. It made me remember the last time we were here, and how I'd watched the goons, then in suits and ties, falling and thrashing around in the water. They didn't seem half as scary then.

As if I'd imagined them to life, they stepped out from behind a couple of giant pine trees.

"Well, look here!" Moose said. "What a connection, meeting you out here."

"It's *coincidence,* dummy," Mikey said.

"That too!"

"And it's not a coincidence; we told them to meet us here!"

Any other time and place, it would have been funny. Now it wasn't.

Then they pulled Aunt Lucy out from behind a tree and pushed her between them.

"Aunt Lucy!" Packrat cried. He rushed toward her, but Mikey held up a hand in a stay-right-where-you-are kind of way. She didn't look hurt, just relieved to see us.

"Sorry, boys; I got caught trying to let the air out of their tires."

I groaned. "I knew we shouldn't have told anyone! This is all my fault."

"You bet it is," Mikey said. "But you can fix it, and then we'll be on our way. Right after you get us the box."

Moose yawned.

"Are we boring you?" Mikey punched him in the arm.

"Sleepy from stealing the eaglet?" Roy asked sarcastically.

"Yeah," Moose said, before opening his mouth to yawn again.

The cry of an eagle circling overhead had him clamping it shut and looking up. It swooped low, casting a shadow over us for a second. Everyone ducked. It cried again, before landing on a branch not too far away. I could see the brown feather on the back of its head. It was the mom eagle.

"Shoo!" Moose said.

"I don't think it works that way, you idiot," Lucy said.

Suddenly, I had an idea. I looked up at the eagle, who was studying us so intently. Then I looked at Mikey. "Where is it?"

He looked confused. "That's what you're going to tell me."

"Not the eagle parts. Where's the eaglet? It has to be here."

"What makes you so sure?"

I nodded toward the eagle. " 'Cause she's waiting to get her talons into you."

Moose looked nervously from me to the eagle. "You mean, attack us?"

Mikey punched him in the arm. "It would have done it already, if it was gonna. It may look tough, but it's just a scared bird, like all other birds. Just flew off to another tree while its baby was being snatched right out of its nest, didn't it? Not even a peck or a scratch."

Moose looked once, twice, from the eagle to a small grouping of young, green pine trees that stood about four feet tall. I cautiously walked toward them, waiting for Mikey to tackle me to the ground, or at least grab me and pull me back. Instead, he shot me a superior grin.

I put my hands into the pines and parted them. Hidden on the ground in the middle of them was a burlap bag. I gently pulled it toward me and rolled the sides down. The fuzzy-headed eaglet blinked several times. For a seven-week-old bird, it was pretty big! The size of a small turkey, its head was as high as my knees. The part-brown, part-fuzzy-gray eaglet sat quietly, staring at me with its brown eyes.

From behind me, Packrat said, "It's not as cute as I thought it'd be."

Roy asked, "Why isn't it trying to get away?"

"It can't fly yet," Gavin said. "In the nest it doesn't move much, because there isn't a lot of room."

I looked up at the mother eagle, willing her to attack Mikey and Moose. But I knew she wouldn't. She hadn't bothered the biologist when his group had banded the eaglets a couple of years ago. The only attack story I'd ever heard was one where a human killed an eaglet and the adult eagle had stalked the killer and messed up his face.

But these goons didn't need to know that.

"Oh, they've been known to attack," I told Moose, straight-faced. "Wait and see. Especially if this baby gets hungry and starts hollering for food."

"I can wait at least five days for that," Mikey said, turning. "Can't I, Gavin?"

I swear my bottom jaw hit the ground. Mikey added, "Oh, we had quite the talk. That's how I knew the eagle wouldn't charge us and I wouldn't have to feed this ugly thing by hand."

I turned to Gavin. Roy rushed past me, but I put an arm out to stop him, wanting to get to Gavin first. "*You* told him that?"

Packrat's eyes were sad. "But why?" he asked.

Roy growled low. He kept clenching and unclenching his fists. "I swore to Cooper you could be trusted! More than once!"

Gavin took a step back and put up both hands. "Really, it's not what you think!" he protested. "I just . . . he . . ." Gavin ducked his head. "He asked. And I didn't think. I just didn't think."

Mikey gripped Lucy's arm harder and shook her until she cried out. "Enough!" he said. "Get the box now."

With one last glare at Gavin, I led everyone to the edge of the canyon where the goons had lost me before. I looked back at Mikey and Moose, hating that I had to show them this.

But maybe it was our way out. These goons were too big to fit down the hole. Or through the gorge in the back. I looked at Lucy. Could she fit?

"It's down there," I said, pointing to the canyon floor. "In a cave."

Mikey's eyes narrowed. "You're lying. There's no way down there. We tried."

You're just too blind to see it." I walked over to the blueberry bushes, parted them, and there was my not-so-secret-anymore entrance. Packrat raised his chin. "I'm sticking with him," he said.

Roy stepped beside him. "Me, too."

Mikey hesitated. Then he nodded. Pointing to Gavin, he added, "He . . ." Then, looking at Lucy, he started again. "*They* stay with us, though."

"You can have him. But we'll be back for her," I said.

I lowered myself down the hole first, into the little cave below. When the three of us were down there, Packrat whispered, "You have a plan, right?"

I shook my head. "Not really, but what else can we do? We've got to give them the parts. I still have the rest of the pictures for proof. We can give them to the warden after we save the eaglet. Besides, there's your aunt Lucy."

Roy agreed.

We shimmied down the tree to get from the cave to the canyon floor. Mikey leaned over the edge to watch us. He gripped Aunt Lucy's arm tightly, to remind us why we needed to go back to the top. I looked longingly toward the gorge—but I couldn't do that to her, or the eaglet.

I followed the canyon wall off to the right until we got to the lower cave. When we stepped into it, the cool, damp air hit us, and so did the semidarkness. We waited for our eyes to adjust.

"Okay, let's grab it, and get back up there," Roy said. "Where'd you stash it?"

I walked to the left side of the cave, to the spot where I'd found a small hole up off the ground. The box had fit just right, and then we'd stuffed a rock in its opening to camouflage it. I wrapped my fingers around the rock and tugged. It didn't give. I put one foot on the canyon wall and pulled with everything I had.

"That's not the spot," Packrat said. He scratched his head. "I think it's more to the right."

Packrat and I started running our hands along every inch of wall, hunting for the loose rock.

"Shoulder-high," I said.

"Waist-high," Packrat said.

"You lost it?" Roy snorted. "Great. Now we have nothing to trade."

In spite of the cool cave air, sweat was beginning to drip down the sides of my face. "It's here!" I insisted.

But what if it wasn't?

What if someone else had found it first?

Chapter 25

*Even though eagles are much smaller than humans,
their eyes are the same size as ours. Although their eyes
can only move a tiny bit, they can rotate their whole
heads 270 degrees.*

"Where'd you go?" Mikey yelled down. The way the canyon wall
slanted in at the bottom, he couldn't see us, even when we stood at the
entrance to the cave.

"We're getting it!" Roy yelled back, as Packrat pulled a flashlight
out of his coat.

"Feel for a wiggly rock," I told my friends.

We each took a separate section of the wall and shoved against
the rocks sticking out of it. I didn't remember there being so many!

Where was it? It shouldn't be this hard! Where was the geocache
box?

"Hurry up!" I heard from overhead.

I closed my eyes and tried to calm down. Clear my head. *You're just
panicking,* I told myself. *We walked in the cave, we went to the left—*

"Got it!" I called, walking straight to a small rock sticking out of
the wall. When I touched it, it wiggled. Pulling the rock from the wall,
I sighed in relief to see the green plastic box stashed inside the dark
opening. I hauled it out and set it on the ground. It took me a minute
to unclasp the large side clip, because my hands were shaking. In fact,
they'd been shaking since the goons had caught me in their motor
home.

"What's taking so long?" Mikey's voice was hard.

Roy stepped back a couple of steps and shielded his eyes from the
sun as he looked up. "Just hold on a minute, wouldya?" He ran a hand
through his hair and muttered, "Sheesh."

It made me feel a little better to know that even Roy was rattled.

We looked again at the eagle parts. Two yellow claws. Two feathers. That old eagle head on the carved handle. I wanted so badly to get these to the warden, but I reminded myself that the eaglet and Aunt Lucy needed to be rescued first.

And yes, Gavin too.

"Let me go! Let me go! *Nooooooo!*" Aunt Lucy's screams from above had us rushing out to look up. "Aunt Lucy!" Packrat cried.

She stood on the very edge of the canyon, trying to back away, but Mikey held her upper arm, crowding her so she leaned sideways over the edge. Only the heel of her right foot was still on the dirt. She tried to grab for Mikey's shirt, but she couldn't quite reach.

One slip and she'd be down with us.

"Don't hurt her!" Packrat cried. "Please! She's got nothing to do with this. We didn't even tell her what was in it!"

I quickly closed the box and pulled it out to where the goons could see it. "Here!" I called. "We've got it! We're coming up."

We climbed the tree one by one, me in the lead. When I reached the upper cave, Moose's head appeared in the hole. I had a quick flash of memory: a book about a giant and a beanstalk. Then his face disappeared and his hand, with a tree trunk of an arm behind it, came down the hole to help me up.

I clutched the box to my chest with one arm and gave him my other hand. He pulled me up like I was a bag of goose feathers.

When I was out of the hole, I stooped to brush the dirt off my knees as the men talked together. I heard Gavin whisper, "You're here!"

A voice shushed him.

Three sets of large-ish hiking boots were before me. *Three?* Two pairs looked new; one was well-worn. My eyes slowly traveled up from the well-worn pair to find Hawke looking back at me. A geocache box lay at his feet. It looked exactly like mine.

"Hey!" I stood straight up, and pointed at the box. "That's the one that went missing on the geocache trail!"

Hawke nodded. "Very good."

I looked daggers at him. He stared calmly back. The more I glared and tried to communicate how mad I was at him for being the boss of these two goons, the calmer his gaze became. Goose bumps popped up on the back of my neck.

"Cooper . . ." Gavin had been so quiet, I hadn't noticed him standing slightly behind Hawke. The man turned and shook his head. Gavin looked at his sneakers.

"Moose, take the box from the kid and bring it here," Mikey said.

Moose had to tug on it twice before I let go. He cradled it in one arm as he turned on his heel to deliver it to Mikey.

"Aunt Lucy, come over here," Packrat called.

But Mikey grabbed Aunt Lucy's arm and hauled her back. He shook a finger at us. "You don't get her until I have it in my hands and make sure it's got our stuff in it. You aren't pulling that one over on us again."

Packrat and Roy started forward, but Mikey put his other hand on his hip where I imagined a gun would be.

Moose was almost to Mikey when he shifted the box from one arm to the other. The lid popped open. The claws and eagle head tumbled to the ground while feathers floated back and forth, once, twice, three times, before settling next to a claw.

Hawke rushed forward. Moose crouched down and started scooping everything up feverishly, as Lucy yelled, "Careful, you fool! Do you want to damage the merchandise?"

Chapter 26

An adult eagle weighs ten to fourteen pounds and has
a wingspan of six to seven feet. The female eagle is
larger than the male.

I gasped and looked at Packrat. He was frozen in place, a disbelieving look on his face. "Aunt Lucy?"

No one heard him. Hawke and Lucy leaned over the eagle parts, carefully arranging them from the pile where Moose had dropped them.

"I'm sorry," Moose pleaded with Lucy. "I didn't know they were fragile."

"Use your head, idiot," Lucy said, not even looking up from her inspection of the eagle head. "You don't just toss a diamond ring or an antique vase, do you?"

Gavin stared at the pieces as if he had found the nest of an extinct bird.

"Aunt Lucy?" Packrat's voice was shaky, but not from fear. He was angry. When she didn't answer, he got louder. "Lucy! What is going on?"

She finally looked his way. Pushing her hair out of her face, she shrugged. "Sorry, kid. I was trying to combine business with pleasure, visiting you and your mom. But these two dummies had to go and put the drop in the middle of your geocache course."

"Is it all here?" Moose asked.

"It is." She sat back on her heels and turned to Hawke. "Do they meet with your approval? Are you still willing to take them off my hands? I'll just need to see the money, of course."

Wait . . . *what?* So, Lucy was the boss and *Hawke* was the buyer!

I looked at Gavin. So what did that make him?

Hawke tapped the decoy geocache box. "It's all in here. I just want to inspect the merchandise first."

Moose reached out between Lucy and Hawke to touch an eagle feather. His hand was slapped sharply by Lucy. Hawke lifted the eagle head on the stick and Mikey leaned down, trying to see the piece better.

All I needed was a couple of minutes . . .

I took a step toward the eaglet. Roy did the same, but Packrat was still staring at Lucy like she had three heads. I tugged on his shirt, once, twice. The third time, he snapped out of it and moved with me.

We took another step. And another.

Gavin caught my eye. He glanced at Lucy and Hawke, then back at me.

Don't do it! I sent the warning with my eyes. Roy clenched his fists, and I heard Packrat suck in a breath.

Gavin mouthed, eyes pleading, *Just stay there.*

I pointed to the eaglet. His brows came together in a frown.

I started backing up slowly. Roy and Packrat stayed close. I kept waiting for Gavin to shout a warning or something, but he didn't. He just got fidgety, like he wasn't sure what to do.

Lucy's attention was totally focused on doing the customer-service thing with Hawke. "This is not how we normally conduct business, you understand. I couldn't think of any other way to get the box back from the kids. Taking the eaglet was the only thing I could come up with to flush them out."

Hawke was still inspecting the box's contents. He held up each feather as if it were a gold bar he was checking for scratches.

Lucy's eyes were fixed on his face. "I wish you hadn't insisted on meeting in person, though. It compromises both of us."

At that, Hawke's lips slowly went upward. "Oh, but I'm very glad to have met the famous boss in person."

Lucy actually giggled as she flipped a piece of hair off her shoulder. "I can't vouch for the kids, but I can assure you—the three of us will never reveal who you are or how you acquired these pieces."

"I certainly hope not." Hawke's smile disappeared, and his deep, soft voice held a hint of warning in it.

I was almost at the eaglet. Almost.

The adult eagle chose that moment to cry out from above. Lucy turned, her eyes scanning the area until they landed on me. "No!"

I sprinted. Having inched my way over, I'd gotten a good head start on everyone else. *The eaglet was mine!*

Suddenly, I found myself falling face-first on the leaf-littered forest floor, musty earth smells up my nose and a long, small log between my feet. "No!" I cried, as Packrat and Roy stopped to help me up. "Go get it!"

But Lucy had already made it to the eaglet. She roughly scooped it up in her arms with a triumphant look.

Packrat and Roy moved toward her, but in a flash, Lucy stood at the canyon's edge. The eaglet struggled a tiny bit, then went still.

"Stay right there," Lucy warned. "Unless you want to see if this baby can fly yet."

"You know it can't!" I cried out. "We had a deal! Give it to me." I reached out my hands.

"I've been thinking," Lucy said, holding the eaglet out in front of her. She inspected its beak and eyes. She took one brown feather on its back and rubbed it between her fingers. "For all the extra time and work I had to put into this job, especially having to climb that tree in the dark and all, I think I'll keep it. A bonus for me!"

Gavin cried out, "Wait!" He grabbed Hawke's arm. "She can't do that!"

Hawke shook off Gavin's arm and shot us both a frustrated look. "I don't know if you've noticed, but she's in charge here."

"You can't keep it! It isn't a pet!" Roy burst out.

Mikey laughed. "She isn't going to keep it for a pet. She'll probably stuff it and sell it to the highest bidder."

Roy gave him one good swift kick in the knee.

"*Oww!*" Mikey raised his hand to hit Roy back. Hawke quickly and silently moved to grab it in midair.

"No need for that," he said. "We'll leave all four of them here, tied up, which gives us all the time we need to get out of town. That will be punishment enough."

"Five," Lucy corrected him. She gave one slow nod to Moose. Before Hawke could blink, Moose had him in a lock-hold.

"Hey! What the—" Hawke struggled, but there was no breaking free of the big, dumb goon.

"I'm getting out of town before you," she explained. "You've seen my face, and I don't want to take a chance you'll double-cross me."

"I know who you are!" Packrat cried.

Lucy smiled sadly. "But you don't know how to find me. I'll go underground. The Lucy you know will vanish. And she won't make the mistake of pretending to visit old college friends again."

"Fine by me," my friend muttered.

"Your coat," Mikey told Packrat. "Put it on the ground. We don't want any funny stuff from you."

Lucy was getting impatient. "Hurry up! Stacey and the other parents might start to wonder where these kids are."

Think! I told myself. *We need a plan!* To my left, Mikey had started to tie up Hawke. Moose, with his arms crossed, stared at Packrat, Roy, and Gavin.

Lucy stood between us and the canyon's edge. I had to get her to put down the eaglet. Give it to me. Something. I just knew I couldn't let her leave with it.

"You'll pay for this!" Hawke warned, as he struggled against the ropes that bound him to the maple tree.

"Careful, or I'll take the eagle parts too," Lucy shot back. "I'm starting to feel a little greedy."

My eyes went to the caches by Mikey's feet. Identical caches. One with the money. One with the parts.

I looked at Gavin. His eyes came up from the cache to meet mine. He mouthed one word.

Manhunt.

I gave a quick nod.

Gavin sucked in a deep breath, then burped a long, loud, from-the-gut *A.*

Lucy whipped his way to stare. Even the eaglet tipped its head to one side at the sound.

I watched every adult like a raptor. Gavin burped the *B.* Hawke looked at him as if he'd lost his mind. Mikey stopped fiddling with the rope to glare over his shoulder.

Three down, two to go.

When Gavin let out with a wicked loud *C,* Moose giggled. "Do the *D.*"

"Stop that!" Lucy yelled.

"Make me," Gavin taunted. He burped an awesomely gross *D.*

"Have you lost your mind, kid?" Mikey clutched the rope in his fist as he moved toward Gavin. "I'm gonna put you next to Hawke there."

Now! I sprinted to the caches, scooped them up, and ran toward the edge of the canyon, well away from Lucy, but where she could see me.

"I'll throw them both over," I cried, "if you don't put down the eaglet."

Lucy stamped a foot. "Why can't you all just behave for two minutes?" she screamed. To her goons, she added, "Don't just stand there—*do* something!"

The goons came for me. "Stop!" I held one hand out over the edge, one of the boxes dangling from it.

"Now, now, don't do anything hasty there," Mikey urged. "Just—"

I held up a box in each hand, raising and lowering them, feeling for the heaviest one. "Hey, Gavin, want some money?" I called, and I tossed one high, right over Mikey's head.

Gavin jumped, catching it with both hands. He shot me a grin.

Lucy gave a frustrated groan. She shifted the eaglet from one arm to the other as she looked between us.

Gavin waved his box back and forth. "I know you want it!"

"Take it!" Lucy cried to the goons. "I don't care what you do, but get that box!"

Mikey and Moose tromped toward him.

"I'm gonna drop mine!" I cried. The goons paused. "If he's got the money, what do you think I have?"

Moose scratched his head, turning toward me, then Gavin, then back to me. "Boss! Which one do you want me to get?"

She was so mad, she couldn't even say the words.

I winked at my friends, calling, "Look!" When Lucy turned, I let the box go for a split second before catching it again.

She gasped and took a step toward me. My friends chuckled. Lucy straightened. She raised her chin.

I warned, "Put down the eaglet and walk away or I'll do it!" I dangled the box again. "I'll drop it!"

"Go ahead," Lucy smirked. "I'll just send you down the hole to get it."

I looked at Gavin, Packrat, Roy, then to Lucy. *What?* Was she bluffing?

I shrugged. "So you don't care if the box falls, breaks open, and the eagle head crashes on the rocks below?" I tossed the box in the air again. Hearing her gasp, I looked at her out of the corner of my eye for a second. And right away, I knew I'd screwed up. The timing was all off now. I reached out to catch it, but it bobbled in my hands. My fingers hit the latch and the box flipped open and spun in midair. Hundred-dollar

bills spilled out and floated everywhere, like snow, down into the canyon.

It was more money than I'd ever seen in one place at one time.

For a second, everyone was totally still, staring as the bills floated silently, landing on rocks, sticking to tree limbs. Then everything happened at once. Mikey and Moose ran to the edge—to do what, I didn't know. It wasn't as if they could catch all that floating money. The box was already on the canyon floor.

When they realized it, they made a grab for me. I dodged.

Lucy screamed, "Get the other box!" The goons gave me one last glare before turning on their heels to look for Gavin, who was already backing away, ready to bolt with the eagle parts.

Roy yelled, "Goons in the hole!" My two crazy friends rushed forward with nothing between them but a long, small log.

"Yeah!" I yelled, punching one fist up in the air. Then I froze. Gavin was between them and the goons. I knew in an instant they'd catch him with the log, too. I took off running, and lunged for his side. I heard Roy's breath in my left ear as I tackled Gavin, then fell in a heap beside him. The end of the log passed so close over my head, it caught a couple of strands of my hair. Packrat's hiking boots pounded past me.

"What the—" Mikey started to say, just as the log hit him and then Moose squarely in the gut, taking the wind out of them both. The surprise and the force of Packrat and Roy behind the log pushed the two goons backward toward the canyon's edge. I knew the minute their feet hit air, because their faces had that *uh-oh* look. Waving their arms and legs, they fell into the canyon.

Crashing sounds, horrible screams of pain, and colorful swearing were all I heard as Gavin and I jumped up and rushed to the canyon's edge to look down along with Roy, Packrat, and Lucy. Down below, Moose sat up, rubbing his head and moaning. Mikey held his wrist, which looked a little crooked. "You'll pay for that!" he called up to us.

Lucy's scream of rage echoed through the woods. She hung the baby over the edge with both hands.

An answering cry rang out.

We'd forgotten her, but now, the mother eagle left her perch to soar straight at Lucy.

Chapter 27

Under their four toes, eagles have small, rough bumps that help them to keep a vise-like grip on the slippery, flapping fish they love to eat.

Lucy ducked and wrapped her arms around her head to protect it from the mother eagle's attack. At the same time, I moved forward to pull Lucy back from the edge of the canyon. The eagle hovered over us, flapping her wings, trying to get at Lucy's head with her long, sharp, black talons and curved yellow beak. The wingspan was so wide, its shadow completely covered us.

I got my hands on the eaglet and tried to pull it toward me. It flapped its wings a little. Lucy's face twisted in anger. "It's mine!" She pulled back.

"You're hurting it!" I shouted.

The adult eagle flew away, but circled around again, this time rearing back, talons out, aiming straight for Lucy's face. With a fierce look, her yellow eyes fixed on Lucy.

Lucy's eyes widened and she shoved the eaglet into my arms. Taking a step back to point at me, she said, "Look! He has it!"

But the eagle kept on course. One razor-sharp talon nicked Lucy's cheek. A tiny bead of blood stood out against her pale, scared face. Lucy took another step backward. Then another. Each one put her closer to the cliff's edge.

Gavin appeared to my left. I thrust the eaglet into his arms, then put out a hand to warn Lucy.

But the eagle suddenly swooped between us, landing in front of her. With its rolling, rocking way of walking, the eagle moved toward Lucy. Hands in front of her face, Lucy screamed, "Help! It's going to kill me!"

"Stand still," I cried. "Make yourself small!" I reached out a hand to calm her.

She took another step back.

"No! Wait!" I began slowly moving around the eagle.

Lucy's back foot stepped onto . . . nothing. She hung there for a second, a surprised look on her face. I rushed forward. Her hands started grabbing at anything within reach—the eagle, a branch, a small tree.

What they caught was my pant leg.

I wasn't expecting it. The weight of that tug brought me down on my butt. I started sliding toward the edge of the cliff in one quick move. The eagle flew off. My feet went over the edge. My ankles. My knees. I couldn't stop myself, and maybe that's why Lucy let go.

I watched as she dropped, arms flailing, hair waving.

It was too late, though. My body was already sliding forward, nothing but open air in front of me, nothing to grab onto. I saw Moose and Mikey sprint to get under Lucy. She fell on them, knocking them over onto their backs for a second time.

I rolled onto my stomach, grabbing at anything I could lay my hands on.

Dirt.

Dirt.

Dirt.

Stick! No—a small pine, growing out of the side of the canyon wall. My hands grabbed hold. They felt like they were on fire as they slid across the rough bark. My body twisted from stopping fast and my back slammed against the canyon wall. A rock jabbed into my lower back, taking my breath away.

There I was, hands above my head, gripping the bottom of the pine, my feet hanging into nothingness. I took a deep breath.

Hearing the flap of her wings, I felt the eagle land above me. I looked up to find her talons wrapped around a branch, only a couple of feet from my eyes. She tipped her white head to look at me with one golden eye.

"Good eagle. Nice eagle," I said. Carefully, I repositioned my hands again. Then I used my feet to turn myself to face the wall. I felt around with one foot for a rock, a branch, a foothold of any kind. The tree slowly tipped toward me. Dirt rained from under the roots, tumbling down the side of the canyon wall onto the goons' heads below. Then small pebbles started rolling out.

"Cooper!" Packrat's voice, from above. "Hold on!"

I couldn't see my friends, but I heard their footsteps moving toward the edge.

"Stop!" Hawke yelled.

"Don't tell us what to do!" Roy shouted angrily.

In a quiet, calm voice, Hawke responded, "If you stand on the edge, your weight will make the tree fall for sure. Packrat, on your stomach, inch forward. Roy, behind him, your hands on his ankles. Gavin, you stand and be the anchor."

"What about the eaglet?" I called up.

"It's safe!" Gavin replied.

I heard the rustle of leaves, and the familiar sound of a coat, sneakers, and knees sliding along the forest floor. How I wished this were a game of Manhunt! I watched as dirt slid out from under the tree's roots, bouncing off my jeans and sneakers to fall to the canyon floor.

Suddenly, my body dropped like I'd been let go. Then I stopped in midair again. Bouncing up and down bungee-style, my stomach did a bunch of flips. I closed my eyes and breathed a sigh of relief. Very carefully, I looked up at the tree.

It hung on by a single root.

The eagle glanced my way with a good-luck-with-that look, then flew off.

A hand appeared over the edge. Fingers wiggled. A second hand appeared, then the face of my best friend.

"Grab on!" Packrat cried. I threw one hand up and he grabbed my wrist with his two hands.

Crack!

The tree pulled out from the wall, tumbling down on Mikey and Moose below. I flung my other hand up to grab Packrat's shirtsleeve.

"Pull!" Packrat cried.

"Pulling!" Roy yelled back.

Small rocks and chunks of dirt crumbled from the edge.

"Move back slowly," Hawke cautioned.

I dug my sneakers into the wall, to help take some of the weight off my friend's hands. Inch by inch I moved up. My foot slipped and I fell face-first into the wall, scraping my cheek. I heard Packrat groan. "It's okay. Gotcha," he said, his voice strained.

Was he trying to reassure me, or himself?

I slid up and up, until finally, I saw Packrat's face all twisted with concentration. He clung to my hand with everything he had, forehead furrowed, sweat running down his temples, skin stretched tight over his shoulders and neck. When my armpits rested on solid ground, Roy grabbed Packrat's shirt and tugged backward, hard. I was dragged up and over the edge.

The three of us fell onto our backs, hands on stomachs, breathing heavily.

"That was close!" Gavin had his hands on his knees, his chest rising and falling. The eaglet sat at his feet. It was panting too, but didn't seem to be in distress. It looked at me, then away again.

"Hey!" Gavin suddenly ran to the edge of the canyon and pointed at the gorge. "Moose is getting away! Through the opening at the back!"

Hawke struggled against the ropes that still bound him to the tree. "Cooper! Your secret entrance! Follow—"

Gavin rushed for the blueberry bushes but stopped, puzzled, when Packrat, Roy, and I began laughing.

"Wait and see," I said. "Moose isn't getting out that way."

Gavin held up his phone. "I'll text my dad to send help. He's waiting."

Roy said to Hawke, "You've got some explaining to do about those eagle parts."

"And the illegal trap you set for the eagle," I added.

Hawke frowned. "Cut me loose, boys. I'll answer all the questions you have about the eagle parts, but what's this about an eagle trap?"

Gavin said, "Cooper, Hawke is—"

Lucy's sharp voice echoed across the canyon. We looked down to see her and Mikey trying to push Moose through the gorge.

"You're too big! Get out and I'll go," Lucy yelled.

But they couldn't pull him out. Moose was stuck.

Chapter 28

In Old English, the word balde *means "white," which is where bald eagles get their name.*

I stood on the far side of the Wentworths' lawn. Well, it's not the Wentworths' anymore, I guess, since there was a bright yellow SOLD sign over the red-and-white FOR SALE one. Whoever the new owners were, I hoped they didn't mind us being here.

Hawke—or Warden Hawke, as it turned out—had just finished putting a red band on the eaglet's right leg.

That's right. Warden Hawke. And not just any warden; he was an undercover warden. When Lucy and her goons had set out to steal some eagle parts to resell on the black market, she'd had no idea that the "little old man she'd taken them from" (her words) was Hawke's grandfather. Hawke had been tracking the three of them for months, trying to get his family's heirlooms back, and to catch them in the act of reselling them. He'd posed as a buyer who was desperate for eagle parts. The hardest thing about the whole undercover operation, he said, was trying to meet the owner face-to-face.

It was the coolest thing I'd ever heard.

"Hand me the silver band," Hawke said. He widened the band to put it around the eaglet's other leg, and used a special tool to secure the band. "The red one, we can spot with binoculars; we know right away it was born in Maine without even seeing the number. The number on the silver one will tell us exactly where and when it was banded, as well as any other information we have."

I looked up at the eagles' nest. Since we'd arrived, both parents had stayed on its edge, watching every move we made. The eaglet with us hadn't made even one little *Hey-where-am-I?* peep. Not when Game Warden Kate had arrived on the scene to cart away Lucy and the goons.

Not when we had carried the eaglet to the canoe. Not when we'd paddled it here. And not since we'd laid it on the blanket so Hawke could get some measurements.

"Might as well, since we have it," he'd said.

Seeing the other three eaglets peeking down at us, I asked, "Will you band the others too?"

"No, just this one. We don't want to be in the nest any more than we have to today."

We crouched around the eaglet. Other than Hawke, the rest of us had been careful not to touch it since we'd left the canyon. There'd been enough of that for one day.

Most of its downy feathers were gone now; the brown plumage it needed to fly, and to stay warm and dry, was taking its place. Large talons poked out from under its body.

"Will you call to tell us the results of the tests you did?" I asked.

"I will," Hawke assured me. We'd checked the eaglet over for injuries, and were surprised to find no broken bones. "This one looks very, very healthy, though."

"Where do your banded eagles end up?" Roy asked.

"All over. They've been found as far away as Virginia." Hawke gently took the eaglet's wing and stretched it out as far as it would go. The eaglet calmly watched as Gavin took a ruler and made measurements—talon width, feather length, and beak length and wrote them all down. Hawke gently guided the wing back against the eaglet's body.

"This eagle family has had enough stress for one season," the warden said. "I think it'd be best if I climb up, put this little fella back in the nest, and get back down as quickly as I can."

Packrat made his hands look like claws. "Won't the parents attack when you get up there?"

"No, but I should have brought my heavy gloves, for handling the talons on this little one. They don't have that much power yet, but those talons are still sharp . . . "

He stopped when Packrat dug into a pocket to pull out a pair of heavy-duty work gloves. Hawke smiled and reached for them. He started to put them on, but stopped. He turned them over and over in his hands, staring at them, thinking.

He passed them to Gavin. "Climb up there with me?"

"Me?" Gavin turned the gloves over and over in *his* hands. "Why?"

"You did a great job monitoring the situation and keeping me in the loop every step of the way."

I gasped. "Gavin was working for *you?*"

"Well, not exactly," Gavin said. His eyes darted from Packrat to Roy, then landed on me. He sighed heavily. "That day I helped you vacuum the pool?"

I nodded for him to go on.

"Before I saw you, I was behind Hawke in line at the store register. He was buying a water hose and a clamp. I saw his warden badge in his wallet. I didn't want to rat you out, Cooper, but I thought if I asked him some questions, it could help me to help you. But then, Hawke asked me to help him and, you know, I ended up being, like, a double agent. The only thing was, you were *both* good guys."

"You were in a tough spot," Hawke said, putting a hand on Gavin's shoulder. "And you did a great job keeping an eye on everyone, including the eagles."

Gavin passed the gloves to me. He looked a surprised Hawke in the eye. "Cooper should be the one to climb up with you. He did all the investigating. He knows way more about eagles than I do. It was his idea to stake out the nest. They would've gotten away with your grandfather's heirlooms, and plus, he saved the eagle from the beaver trap—"

Hawke held up a hand. "That's right! You mentioned a trap earlier?"

"Yes," I said. "Someone caught a beaver in a trap and—"

My friends all talked over each other to tell the story, including the part where we thought the trap had been placed there to catch an eagle, but Game Warden Kate had told us that Lucy and the goons didn't know anything about it.

The warden frowned. "That would be poaching this time of year."

Gavin added, "Cooper was the hero that day, too. He's the one who put Packrat's coat over the eagle to quiet it, then he sprung it free."

Hawke studied me for a minute. I tried not to squirm under his gaze. Finally, he handed me the gloves.

"Really?" I asked. Those gloves were like gold to me.

He turned to a giant bag I'd noticed when we'd all hiked out of the canyon and gotten back in our kayaks and canoes. "I always keep two sets of climbing equipment," he explained. "Just in case."

First, he pulled out a thick, brown harness. Putting it around my waist, he clipped it, and tightened it. I moved it around. It was loose, but not so loose that it'd slide down my hips.

"How does it feel?" he asked.

"Good!" If it were falling off me, I still would have said it was fine.

I watched Hawke put on his own harness, then copied him when he wrapped the leg straps around his upper thighs and buckled them.

Next, he gave me two J-shaped, metal things. Each had one buckle at the top and one near the bottom. "These are our spikes," he said.

Gavin stepped forward to help me. He held the spikes so the bottom of the J's were facing in opposite directions. "Step on them," he said. He reached out to make sure my sneaker was in the right spot, then he fastened the buckles on the outside of my legs. "You should be wearing boots, but you'll be okay."

Each of the spikes was on the inside of my foot, pointing down. It felt a little weird.

Gavin stood up. "You're good to go."

"Hey," I said. "Thanks."

"For what?"

"For calling Hawke to come to the canyon . . . for—"

"Calling Hawke? I didn't call and rat you out. Lucy set that up. I just thought we were handing over the box for the eaglet. Clean and simple."

"Oh! I thought . . ." My ears turned red, and I bent to pretend-fix a buckle on the spikes. Now he'd know I thought he'd ratted us out. "You know, 'cause you're on your phone a lot . . ."

Gavin laughed. "That? Ha! Usually, it's my dad." Gavin shook his head. "It's a real pain, you know. I'm almost eighteen, and he still makes me check in."

I grinned. Yeah. I knew what that was like. "Still, thanks for having my back."

Gavin gently pushed my shoulder. "Anytime."

"Cooper." Hawke's voice brought us back to his side. He put each of his pointer fingers through the metal loops on the harness at his hips. "These are how we attach our rope; we call it a lanyard." He pulled two ropes from the bag and handed me one. It was thicker than a regular rope, and stiffer too. It didn't flop around so much. Each end had a metal clip; one of them he clipped to my harness.

"I get it!" I grinned at him, and threw the other end of the rope around the tree to clip it to the other loop on my harness. I leaned back to put weight on the rope, and started to put a spike on the tree to raise myself up.

"You'll need another for safety," Hawke warned. Hooking another rope clip to the metal loop on my left, he walked the rope around the tree to hook it on the other side of my harness as well. "One rope should always be about shoulder-height on the tree, and the other, lower. Lean back to keep the ropes tight on the tree; lean forward to loosen them, and move them up as you go."

I looked straight up and gulped in some air.

"We're lucky," Hawke said, putting one hand on my shoulder and pointing up the tree trunk with the other. "This pine doesn't have a lot of branches to work around.

"As you climb, be sure to keep your spikes in, legs apart, and lean back for support. To move up, lean in toward the tree, and flip the rope up. Lean back to take some more steps up." He made eye contact with me and asked, "Still good?"

For an answer, I grabbed hold of the rope and started to climb. Lean in, flip up the rope, lean back, take steps up. I'd gone up only three feet when Hawke called, "Looking good! Hold there and I'll get the eaglet."

I leaned back to look down. Hawke lifted the eaglet off the ground and showed it off to my friends one last time.

"See ya around the lake," Packrat said.

"Leave some fish for me," Roy added.

Gavin held out a burlap bag. Hawke gently put the eaglet in. If someone tried to put me in a burlap bag, I know I would have kicked and screamed. But not this eaglet. Hawke then drew the bag closed and attached a rope to it. The other end of the rope was attached to his harness.

"Ready?" Hawke said from underneath me.

"Ready," I said.

Chapter 29

*When soaring, eagles can spot a fish or a rabbit up to a
mile away.*

I took a deep breath and tried to find a rhythm to the climb. Two
steps up, legs apart, spikes in the tree, lean in, slide the rope up, lean
back, and take two steps up again.

At first I had to repeat every move in my mind, but before I knew it,
I could do it without thinking. I heard Hawke behind me, his spikes stick-
ing in and being pulled from the tree, his rope scraping along the bark.
It made me feel better, knowing he was there.

At fifteen feet up, Packrat's excited voice drifted up from below. I
looked down, surprised to see how small he'd gotten already. I followed
his pointer finger to find the adult eagles soaring away from the nest.

I looked down at Hawke. "Should we go back down? Did we scare
them off for good?"

"It happens every time," he assured me. "They'll be back as long as
we're not here too long."

Putting one foot above the other again, I found myself moving
pretty quickly. When I came to a branch, I'd stop, unhook one rope from
my harness to bring it up over the branch, and re-hook it. Then I'd move
the other rope.

Before I knew it, I was under the nest. It was ginormous! It sat like
an upside-down umbrella over my head. I was completely in the shade.

Hawke's head was about at my waist, and to my left. He adjusted
his ropes, then leaned back to take the eaglet's bag off his hip.

"Find a spot where you can get your head and shoulders above the
side of the nest. I'll pass the bag to you so my weight isn't on the tiptop
of this tree."

Pass the bag to me? *Me?* What if I dropped it?

I froze. I couldn't do this! What was I thinking? Hawke should be up here! Gavin! Packrat with all his gadgets. Or Roy; he was braver and tougher than me.

Encouraging calls drifted up from down below. Packrat jumped up and down in a you-can-do-it-dude kind of way. Roy shaded his eyes with one hand and gave me a thumbs-up with the other. Gavin, though, was gazing out over the lake. I shifted to look that way too. A tiny Mom and Dad and a waving Molly were arriving in a toy-size motorboat. Gavin's dad and Packrat's mom were in another.

Uh-oh. Busted.

Something rustled over me. Small pieces of grass and bark fell on my head. Climbing a little higher, I looked up at the underside of the nest, and found one side that wasn't sticking out quite as far as the rest. I turned my body until I was under that section, and shimmied up. With the last step, my head and shoulders rose above the side of the nest.

I was nose-to-nose with an eaglet. Two eaglets, actually. The third was pulling himself across the nest with his beak.

I bent my knees a little. When Hawke handed up the bag, I rested it there so I could use two hands to open it. Leaning way back in the harness, I opened the bag as wide as I could. The eaglet just walked right out, then turned around and looked at me. It poked my hand with its brown beak, then sat straight up, blinking as it looked around.

Knowing I'd probably never get to be this close to an eagle nest again, I took a minute to check it all out. The nest was filled with mostly sticks and moss. Bones everywhere! I grabbed about ten different kinds, plus a couple of feathers, and put them in the bag. I thought Hawke might like to have them for research.

Hearing the sound of grinding gears, I turned toward the Wentworths' house. A moving van was backing into the driveway.

Time to head back down.

"Stay safe, you guys," I whispered. "Watch out for raccoons."

One foot under the other. Lean in, slide one rope down, then the other. Only once did my foot slip. Mom gasped. I could hear it all the way up the tree. Hawke rappelled down, staying beneath me. Dad got under me too, on the ground.

Molly cupped both hands around her mouth and cried out, "Careful, Cooper!"

I never felt like I was going to fall. The harness and ropes kept me in place.

When I got within a couple of feet from the ground, I loosened the ropes and scooted down the tree.

Mom rushed over, her arms out for an unavoidable hug. "Cooper! Are you okay?"

I squirmed away to grin up at her. "That . . . was . . . so . . . *cool!*"

Gavin's dad had a hand on his son's arm while he laughed with Hawke. I found out, after we'd cut Hawke free from the tree, that Hawke had asked Mr. Valley to be on the lookout for his heirlooms when he went antiquing in the area, just in case Lucy was lying about the box being stolen, and had sold them for more money instead. It was Mr. Valley who'd found the tomahawk I'd seen lying on the bed in Hawke's camper, and reported it to him. It didn't belong to Hawke's family, but he'd bought it anyway, to take back to his grandfather as a surprise. Now he had the rest of their heirlooms, too.

Packrat was squirming in his mother's tight hug. "Really, Mom! It's okay!" he kept telling her over and over.

"I should never have let Lucy stay in our motor home!" she wailed, pushing Packrat away from her. "I hadn't seen her since college." She pulled him back in to put her chin on his head. "A clothing buyer for HP Fashions? What a liar!"

Mom grabbed both sides of my face so she could look me in the eye. "What happened here?" She ran a finger over the scratch on my cheekbone. "Did those guys . . . I swear, I don't know what I'd . . ." Eyes welling up, she dragged me in for another bone-crushing hug.

"Ouch!" Moms. Sheesh.

I glanced at Roy, who was standing by himself, expecting to see him make fun or something. Instead, he looked at me quickly, then looked away.

Huh.

Molly hugged both Mom and me around the waist. "I didn't get to see the baby! Cooper, you never wait for me!"

"I took pictures for you," Packrat said. He dug into a pocket to pull out his camera and show her. "Here's Cooper holding—"

An eaglet shrieked. Then another. Pretty soon all four had their heads high, looking off across the lake as they bellowed.

"Will the adults come back?" I asked Hawke, as we all gathered around to watch.

"Oh, yes. Usually within a couple of hours."

A dark blue sports car blaring old rock music like the kind my dad liked pulled into the Wentworths' driveway. I thought two things. One: That was a cool car! But two: It wasn't a family car.

Dad clapped a hand on my shoulder. "Wow! So what was it like up there?"

"The nest is way bigger than it seems. Oh! And I found some stuff in it." I handed the bag to Hawke. "I thought you might like it."

Dad hooked a thumb back toward the car. "I expect a full report on the boat ride back. But first, I'm going to introduce myself to our new neighbors, and let them know what's going on."

New neighbors? I looked again. A girl with long blonde hair, wearing jeans and a baseball cap, stood looking up at the sky. She leaned over to say something to the driver, then pointed up.

Gavin shouted, "Look!"

Soaring over the treetops, one of the adult eagles was making its way back toward the nest. Suddenly, it dove to snatch a fish from the lake's surface and rose back into the air in one quick move. It circled the nest once, before dropping the trout to its young, waiting eagerly below. As it perched on a nearby branch, the other eagle flew in with something furry.

We all watched the biggest eaglet pull itself over to the meal.

"Go on," Packrat coaxed. "Take a big bite."

The eaglet pecked. Then it dug in, while the others started crying for food. The parents nudged the food around. When the others kept crying, they started to feed them.

"Another adventure, another family saved," Packrat said, clapping a hand on my shoulder. "I wonder what we'll find next."

One of the eaglets stretched its wings and caught the wind, talons lifting off the nest for a second. Could there be a cooler adventure than saving a baby eagle?

"I don't know," I said. "But I can't wait!"

Author's Note

Dear Reader,

Whether you treasure-hunt on busy city streets or on peaceful mountaintops, geocaching is a wonderful sport! It puts you outside and gets your feet moving and your brain thinking. The thrill of the hunt takes you on trails and to places you've never visited before. Some might even be located just a few miles from you.

Caches come in a variety of sizes and are hidden in remarkable locations by some very creative geocachers. My family's most difficult—and most rewarding—find was a tiny, magnetic screw placed through the leg of a hiking-trail sign. Once we twisted off the top of the screw, the base held the tiniest roll of paper we'd ever seen.

To find out more about geocaching, especially how to get started, I recommend visiting www.geocaching.com.

Should you accidentally find a cache, please leave it where it lies. That's what Cooper and Packrat would do . . . although they'd probably sign the logbook first.

Tamra Wight

Acknowledgments

In 2005, on a day in June, a man drove into our campground and asked permission to launch his boat into Lower Range Pond. Seeing a motor larger than 9.9 horsepower, I told him in no uncertain terms that it was "too big for our lake."

"I have permission from the wardens," he said, pulling out his card. Bill Hanson was a senior biologist, sent to band the eaglets.

"Would you like to come along?" he graciously asked.

I grabbed my camera and followed; I didn't even think twice. Didn't stop to close or lock the door to the campground office, either.

Watching Chris, Rick, and Jesse measure the feathers and talons of two eaglets for a couple of hours, as Bill sat at the top of the tree, raising and lowering them, I knew it was too cool an experience not to share in a book someday.

Like Bill and his team, so many people helped to inspire and create *Mystery of the Eagle's Nest* along the way. Indulge me, please, while I thank a few of them here. If I forget anyone, please know it was by accident. As always, I'm grateful to each and every one of you.

Since that day in 2005, I've kept close watch over our nesting eagle pair. Each February is spent snowshoeing down to the point with my dog Cookie, large camera around my neck, anxiously seeking signs the pair has reunited. Early in March, I hope to see them mating. Late March, they're sitting on the eggs. April brings signs the chicks have hatched. But the most exciting time is early May, when the campers and I train our cameras, binoculars, and even the occasional telescope on the nest for a glimpse of chick heads bobbing up and down.

"How many will there be?" is always the question of the year. Will they all survive? When will they branch? Fledge? Thank goodness my campers keep me well informed (especially my young ones) as I spend more and more time in the store instead of on my beloved lake. I live for their updates, and many of their observations made it into this book.

In 2012, we were blessed to witness the arrival of triplets. After the last eaglet fledged, the eight-hundred-plus-pound nest fell over. All fall, my Poland Spring Campground campers mourned, but none more so than the seasonal kids. I was peppered with questions: "Will the eagles re-nest? Can't we do anything? Call someone? What about a platform?"

That November, my husband and I saw signs of rebuilding. I actually had tears in my eyes as I wrote the blog post to report it: The eagles were re-nesting in the exact same spot! Obviously they liked their location as much as we do!

Even with all of my firsthand research, and that of my campers, I couldn't have gotten all the little details right without the expertise of Chris DeSorbo, Raptor Program Director, Biodiversity Research Institute; copy editor Melissa Hayes, and the rest of the Islandport staff. I especially appreciate my patient and talented editor, Melissa Kim, who always asks just the right making-me-think-and-dig-just-a-little-bit-deeper questions. Creating a book is a team effort, and I can't adequately express how fortunate I feel to be a part of this one.

Carl DiRocco, your illustrations have rendered me speechless (which is not easy to do!). The curve of the wings, the expressions, the action . . . so perfect. Thank you.

Behind the scenes, I've had the unconditional support of the teachers, students, librarians, and the administration of Maine's RSU 16, especially Bruce M. Whittier and Poland Community School. Can I just publicly say, you're an amazing group of educators and a super-smart student body. I brag about you all. A lot.

Once again, my circle of online and in-person writing friends have "had my back" while I was writing *Mystery of the Eagle's Nest*, from early-draft readings back in 2011, to advice and encouragement through the last few months of revisions. I'm one lucky writer to be surrounded by such giving authors, so gifted in their craft. A special shout-out goes to my Camp 'n Schmooze attendees: Cindy Lord, Carrie Jones, Val Giogas, Mona Pease, Jo Knowles, Denise Ortakales, Cindy Faughnan, Mary Morton Cowan, Laura Hamor, Jeanne Bracken, Nancy Cooper, Anna Boll, and Joyce Johnson. Without our biannual meetings, I might have given up long ago.

No one shouts encouragement louder than my family, though. Mom and Dad, in-laws Ron and Lee, my sisters and brother, all the in-laws (and outlaws), seventeen nieces and nephews, umpteen aunts and uncles, a gazillion cousins—I heard you all the way up here in Maine, and it made me smile.

Alex, I'll never forget the day we made our huge eaglet discovery! How we kept looking through the camera lens to count the little gray heads over and over, until we had picture-perfect proof of triplet eaglets. It's one of my favorite mother-daughter memories.

Ben, remember the first geocaches we found? Searching in stone walls, cellar holes, and old rotted tree stumps? My favorite is still the canyon, though, where the coordinates took us to its edge and you discovered the secret entrance to the floor. Never lose that sense of adventure. It will take you places.

And once again, last but not least, thank *you*, David. My proofreader, my cheerleader, my rock, my partner, my heart. This publishing adventure is all the more fun with you beside me.